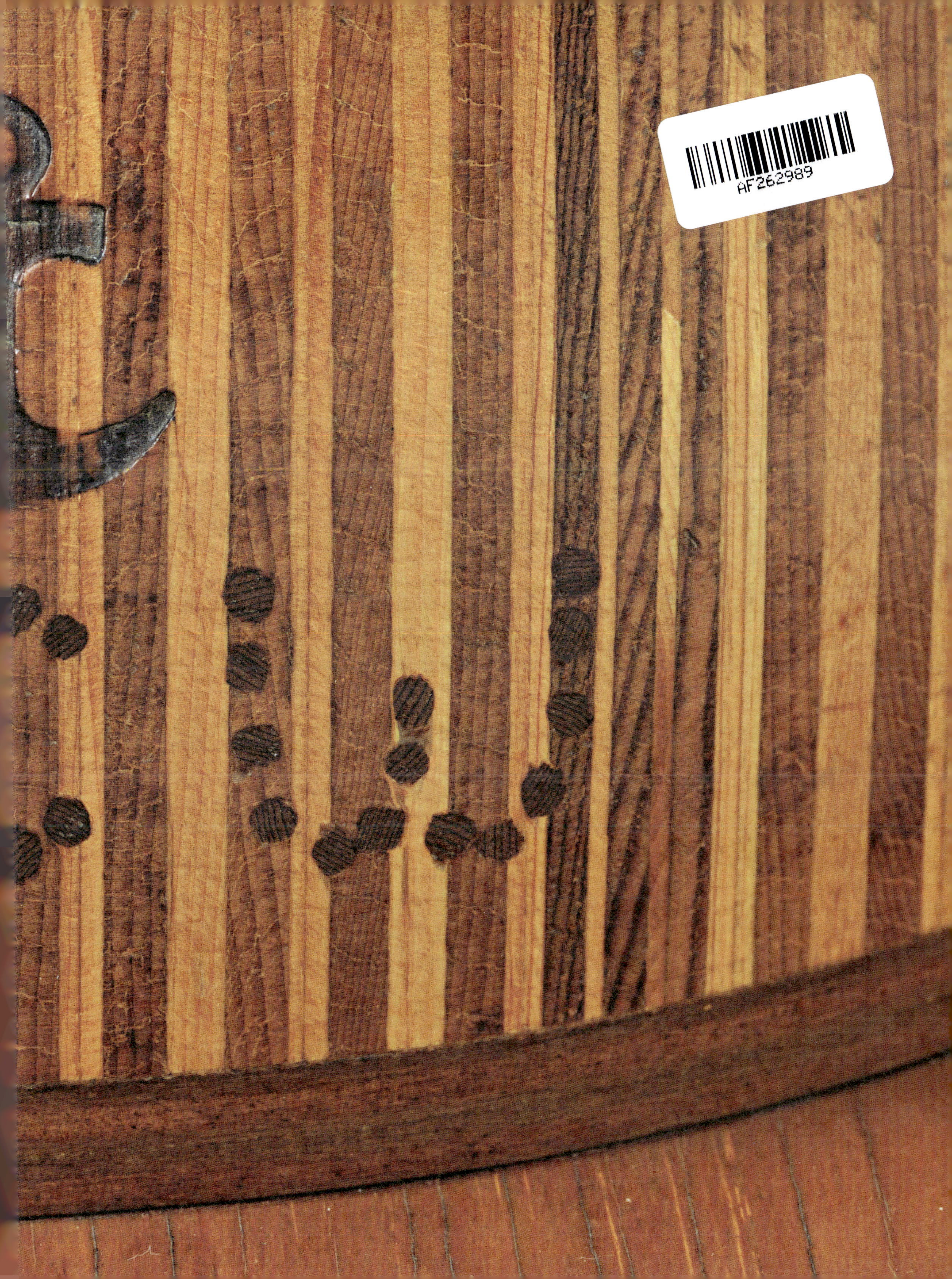

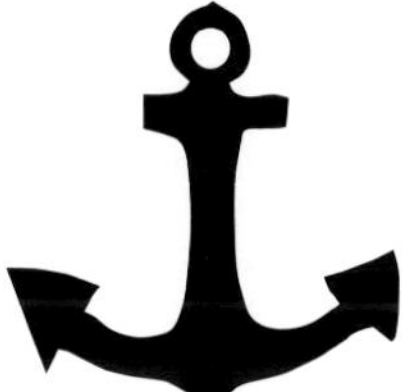

H. C.
WESTERMANN

EDITED BY GIAMPAOLO BIANCONI

WITH ESSAYS BY
GIAMPAOLO BIANCONI AND THEA LIBERTY NICHOLS
AND AN INTERVIEW WITH ED RUSCHA

ANCHOR CLANKER

THE ART INSTITUTE OF CHICAGO

DISTRIBUTED BY YALE UNIVERSITY PRESS,
NEW HAVEN AND LONDON

CONTENTS

6   A NOTE ON ALAN AND DOROTHY PRESS

7   FOREWORD

8   ACKNOWLEDGMENTS

10   **MARLON BRANDO IN DRAG**
      GIAMPAOLO BIANCONI

20   **MY COMIC BOOK HERO**
      ED RUSCHA WITH GIAMPAOLO BIANCONI

28   **"SINCERELY, CLIFF": WESTERMANN AND THE NEW GENERATION**
      THEA LIBERTY NICHOLS

40   PLATES

106   LIST OF WORKS

108   CONTRIBUTORS

109   INDEX

A NOTE ON ALAN AND DOROTHY PRESS

THE ART INSTITUTE OF CHICAGO IS THE BENEFIciary of and home to a recent gift from the stellar art collection of Alan and Dorothy Press, which reflects the couple's keen eye, love of travel, and lasting relationships with artists and curators in Chicago and beyond. Throughout their marriage, Alan and Dorothy acquired significant works by artists such as Philip Guston, Henri Matisse, Ken Price, Ed Ruscha, and, of course, H. C. Westermann, the focus of the exhibition presented at the Art Institute from May 2025 to May 2026. For more than forty years, Alan and Dorothy helped the museum acquire more than fifty works of art, an awe-inspiring demonstration of philanthropy that culminated in 2023 with this monumental gift of seventeen iconic sculptures by Westermann.

The personal spirit of connection between this remarkable couple and the enigmatic artist has informed much of the content of this book, which aims to reflect Alan and Dorothy's intimate understanding of these objects and their maker. Alan was direct and plainspoken, capturing the intersection of the couple's friendship with Westermann and his works, writing to the artist, "Our pieces…took on added dimension: your personality and character reinforced and added to our perception of them."

Alan and Dorothy's children, Steven Goldberg, Richard Goldberg, Steven Press, Clayton Press, and Lauren Press, honored their parents' wishes and legacy by gifting these Westermann sculptures to the Art Institute. The museum is honored to publish and exhibit the Alan and Dorothy Press Collection and appreciates both the vision of these extraordinary partners and collectors and this opportunity to share their philanthropy with the public.

FOREWORD

"EVEN IN HIGH SCHOOL IN LA, HE HAD HIS EYE on the Art Institute of Chicago," wrote Joanna Beall Westermann of her husband not long after his death in 1981. She continued in her letter to A. James Speyer, the museum's curator of twentieth century art at the time, "I'm very glad he got there. I know he was." During the years H. C. Westermann called Chicago home, he studied at the School of the Art Institute of Chicago and earned the respect of younger artists in the city whom he later called friends. Although he gained admiration from artists, curators, and critics in New York, Los Angeles, and Europe, to this day Westermann is most strongly associated with Chicago. The artist's deadpan humor, homespun surrealism, workhorse dedication to craft and material, and individualist personality all testify to the city's history of fearless artistic experimentation.

This publication celebrates Alan and Dorothy Press's remarkable gift of seventeen Westermann sculptures to the Art Institute of Chicago. The pieces not only span his entire career but also represent key bodies of his work, solidifying the museum's reputation as a center for the appreciation, dissemination, and study of the artist's singular art. This addition to our collection is the culmination of a decades-long institutional collaboration that spans many colleagues, past and present, and builds upon the Press's earlier generous donation of thirty Westermann works on paper.

I sincerely thank Steven Goldberg, Richard Goldberg, Steven Press, Clayton Press, and Lauren Press for entrusting their parents' exceptional collection of Westermann works to the Art Institute, and I express my deep gratitude to their legal counsel, Alexandra Darraby, for her support of this project. The extraordinary philanthropy of the Press family has augmented gifts by other patrons, including Edwin and Lindy Bergman, Henry and Gilda Buchbinder, and Lewis Manilow, artists Cynthia Carlson and Robert Bertoletti, artists Jim Nutt and Gladys Nilsson, Westermann's dealer Allan Frumkin, and Anstiss and Ronald Krueck. Their contributions have steadily increased Westermann's presence in our collection over the decades.

For his role in bringing together this catalogue and exhibition, I congratulate Giampaolo Bianconi, Dittmer Associate Curator, Modern and Contemporary Art, who led a talented and dedicated group of colleagues within and beyond this institution. This project not only provides a much-needed contemporary resource on Westermann that will last beyond our time but also celebrates the Press family's crucial role in the art history of Chicago.

I reserve my greatest admiration for Westermann himself—the exquisite craftsman, linguistic (and literal) gymnast, and endlessly fascinating artist whose work still retains the power to entrance viewers and reconstruct the dominant narratives of twentieth-century art.

James Rondeau
President and Eloise W. Martin Director
The Art Institute of Chicago

ACKNOWLEDGMENTS

FOREMOST THANKS ARE DUE TO ALAN AND Dorothy Press, who assembled this extraordinary collection of H. C. Westermann's work, and to their children, Steven Goldberg, Richard Goldberg, Steven Press, Clayton Press, and Lauren Press, who fulfilled their parents' intention to donate this body of sculpture to the Art Institute of Chicago. The execution of this generous gift testifies to the vision of James Rondeau, President and Eloise W. Martin Director, whom I wish to thank for entrusting me with the presentation of these works in this publication and in our galleries. Jennifer Sostaric, Senior Associate General Counsel, and Jay Dandy, Collection Manager, Modern and Contemporary Art, were instrumental in executing the gift and offered support throughout.

H. C. Westermann: Anchor Clanker has benefited from the extraordinary guidance of Sarah Guernsey, Deputy Director and Senior Vice President for Curatorial Affairs and Interim Chair of Modern and Contemporary Art, for which I am most grateful. Equally crucial has been the leadership of Sarah Kelly Oehler, Vice President of Curatorial Strategy and Field-McCormick Chair and Curator, Arts of the Americas; David Nacol, Senior Vice President, Philanthropy; Katie Rahn, Senior Vice President, Marketing and Communications; Emily Benedict, Vice President, Campus Operations; Amy Allen, Vice President, Engagement; and Aaron Anderson, Associate Vice President, Financial Planning and Analysis. Henry and Gilda Buchbinder opened their home and collection to me early in this process. Leslie Buchbinder's interest in and attention to all things Westermann provided critical context for this project. Throughout the planning of this catalogue and exhibition, I have been honored by the generous counsel, encouragement, and expertise of Ann Goldstein, Deputy Director and Senior Curator at Large.

In Chicago, I have been honored by the friendship of Susanne Ghez, Anne Rorimer, and John Vinci. Their perspectives on Westermann helped inform this publication. Elisabeth Sussman, Sondra Gilman Curator of Photography at the Whitney Museum of American Art, spent a memorable afternoon with me discussing Westermann and his universe. At the Art Institute, Mark Pascale provided valuable insights throughout the project.

For their contributions, I thank Ed Ruscha, who generously shared his insights, memories, resources, and Thea Liberty Nichols, who graciously lent her expertise on Chicagoland artists, augmented by her exchanges with Sarah Canright, Cynthia Carlson, Art Green, Gladys Nilsson, and Jim Nutt. Mary Dean of the Ruscha Studio was a gracious partner and connected me with the wonderful Wendy Al Bengston, who introduced me to special photographs that capture her and Billy Al Bengston's friendship with the artist. Harrison Sherrod of Pentimenti Productions also helped us access images and archives.

Without the assistance of my capable colleagues in Modern and Contemporary Art, now led by Paulina Pobocha and including Annika M. Bohanec, Jay Dandy, and Makayla May, this book—and countless other projects—would not have come to fruition. Isabella Diefendorf was steadfast in her research and role as an interlocutor. I am indebted to Nicholas Barron and Christina Warzecha for their sensitive attention to and movement of these works (and so much more). Joanna Abijaoude, Caitlin Haskell, Alivé Piliado Santana, and Tamar Kharatishvili also provided crucial support and encouragement.

The Publishing team, led expertly by Katie Reilly, shepherded this book to completion, and for that I am immensely grateful. Ben Bertin and then Lauren Makholm handled the production, with essential support from Isella Sandoval, and Josephine Yanasak-Leszczynski diligently managed images and image rights. Sheila Majumdar edited the manuscript with great skill and creativity, with guidance from Lisa Meyerowitz. Bonnie Rosenberg led the team in Imaging; Nathan Keay, Robert Lifson, Jonathan Mathias, Juan Molina Hernández, and Joe Tallarico provided outstanding photography; Elyse M. Allen spearheaded production; and Kaitlyn Fultz-Campion deftly completed "Operation Peanut" and shined in post-production. Beverly Joel of pulp, ink. conceived of and executed the elegant publication design.

No undertaking of this import is possible without the contributions of many individuals across the museum. Kendall McElhaney was attentive and fastidious in planning and executing this exhibition. Samantha Grassi dealt gracefully with the gallery's space and volume, ensuring an engaging and accessible presentation. Haddon Dine cared for Westermann's works with the skill and dedication she brings to all projects. Andy Talley constructed several mounts to elegantly display the sculptures. Ginia Shubik Sweeney shaped the interpretation of artworks for our visitors, with help from Sheila Majumdar, and Layne Thue-Bludworth ensured the graphic design was clear and refined. Facilities and Logistics, led by Thomas Ryan, and Protection Services, under Lucio Ventura, secured the safe presentation of works. Colleagues in Visitor Engagement, headed by Peter Smiler, ensured that audiences experienced a warm welcome and stimulating visit.

Everyone who contributed to this project proved their devotion to H. C. Westermann, letting his spirit guide the making of this accessible catalogue and accompanying exhibition. We are proud to present the artist's work—deeply respected and admired in his lifetime—to an ever-broadening audience of artists, scholars, and the public.

Giampaolo Bianconi
Dittmer Associate Curator, Modern and Contemporary Art
The Art Institute of Chicago

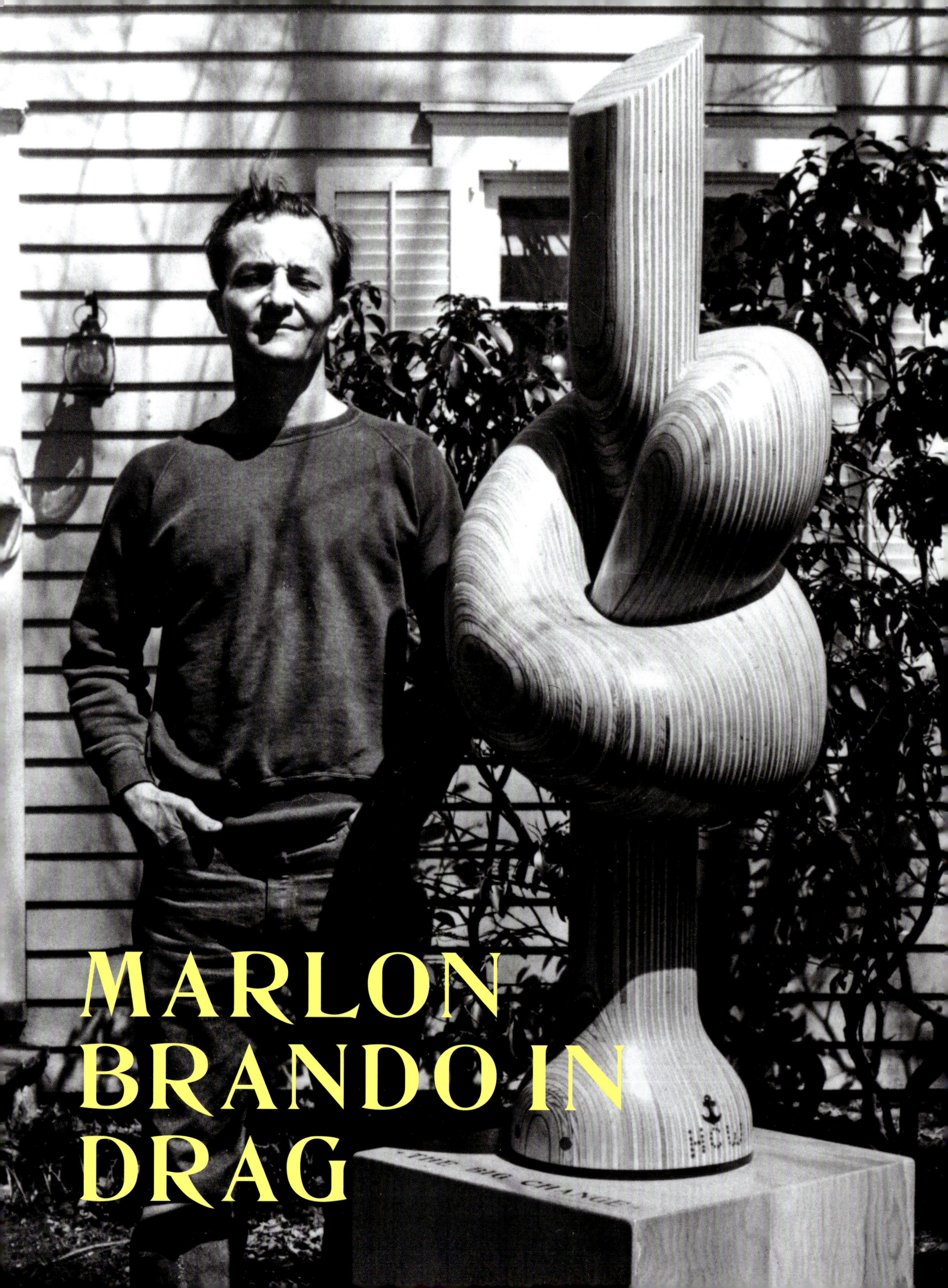

MARLON
BRANDO IN
DRAG

GIAMPAOLO BIANCONI

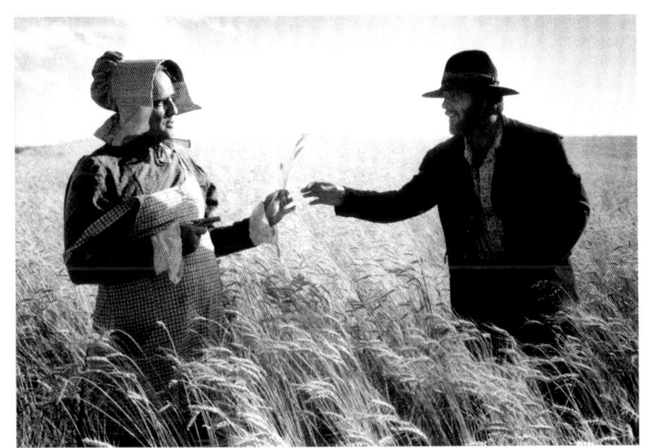

IN 1976 ED RUSCHA SENT H. C. WESTERMANN A LETTER ABOUT A FILM HE just watched. "I saw a movie tonight called *Missouri Breaks*," wrote Ruscha to the older artist, "Why didn't you tell me you were Marlon Brando in drag?"[1]

In the film, Brando plays a gun for hire in the Old West who signs up to neutralize a gang of cattle raiders on behalf of a wealthy land baron. He dons a number of disguises throughout, in one scene wearing a pinafore and a bonnet (see fig. 1). Brando dressed as a woman numerous times during his career and would show up around town to give acting classes in drag. For an actor who made his name as the ur-masculine protagonist in *A Streetcar Named Desire* (1951) and *On the Waterfront* (1954), adopting the appearance of a woman likely offered a form of freedom and liberation from the oppressive performance of traditional gender roles.

"You should see this picture," continued Ruscha, "just to see how closely this character is aligned with yours and your work (and I'm not just making wind). You will be surprised. I'm sure." Lest his message not be fully absorbed, Ruscha included a postscript after his signature: "P.S. SEE THE MOVIE."[2]

The Missouri Breaks—which paired Brando with Jack Nicholson, fresh off of his Academy Award–winning turn in *One Flew Over the Cuckoo's Nest* (1975)—was a critical and commercial flop. Writing in the *New York Times*, critic Vincent Canby characterized Brando's performance as "out-of-control," continuing, "He enters the film hidden behind a horse, which he at last peeks around, and then spends the rest of the movie upstaging the writer, the director and the other actors. Nothing he does…has any apparent connection to the movie that surrounds him. He grabs our attention but does nothing with it."[3]

Ruscha presumably had other qualities in mind than those noted by Canby. But the critic's assessment at least offers a starting point for considering such a comparison: Westermann certainly upstaged everyone around him, despite a lack of entrepreneurial ambition. He also sought to escape from the tenets of American life that shaped his youth, specifically violence and war. Aside from being a talented woodworker and inspired artist, Westermann joined the Marines, worked on railroads, performed as an acrobat, supported himself as a carpenter, and was known among his friends for his

1. Ed Ruscha, letter to H. C. Westermann, May 16, 1976, H. C. (Horace Clifford) Westermann Papers (c. 1925–1982), Archives of American Art, aaa.si.edu/collections /hchorace-clifford-westermann-papers-9345 (hereafter Westermann Papers, AAA).

2. Ibid.

3. Vincent Canby, "'Missouri Breaks,' Offbeat Western," *New York Times*, May 20, 1976, 44.

impressive ability to walk on his hands. But square jaw, sharp chin, muscular physique, and extensive tattoos aside (see fig. 2), his physical machismo belied a sensitive and warm interior life shaped as much by his lifelong desire to be an artist as by his experiences in the Pacific theater of World War II and in the Korean War.

Westermann's sculptures are likewise characterized by the tension between interior and exterior. Take *The Mysteriously Abandoned New Home* (fig. 3), the first Westermann work acquired by the Art Institute of Chicago in 1962. The sculpture—a closed octagonal structure that is somehow both a church and a missile—is as precisely crafted as any by the artist, bearing almost no exterior trace of his labor. It is virtually seamless; yet Westermann included numerous points of potential access. A seemingly functional hinged door is boarded up, as is a window, and a couple of other windows offer glimpses of the empty interior. When first exhibited, the work was even accompanied by a step stool that allowed visitors to peer inside more easily. Writing about Westermann's work in the late 1970s, critic Donald Kuspit described the artist's central concerns as the navigation of public and private, personal and collective, and throughout his works, finely wrought exteriors are outfitted with doors and portals that open onto nothing.[4]

Westermann's experiences in the military led him to explore this tension—and the senseless emptiness of war. He enlisted in the United States Marine Corps in 1942, serving on the USS *Enterprise* in World War II, an iconic vessel that earned the moniker "Galloping Ghost" for its ability to withstand heavy damage and remain afloat; in at least one instance when Westermann was aboard, the aircraft carrier was attacked and later erroneously reported as sunk. A newspaper profile of him as a young corporal describes numerous brushes with death, one a result of pure chance: from about one hundred feet above the deck, a Japanese plane dropped a five-hundred-pound bomb directly onto the ship. Incredibly, "the bomb hit tail first and knocked off the fuse, rendering it harmless."[5] What could

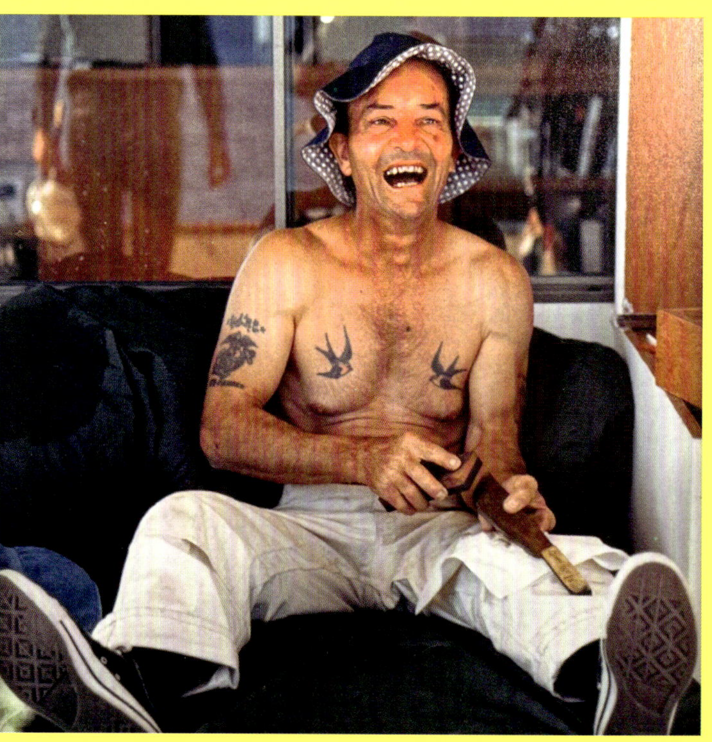

FIG. 2
H. C. WESTERMANN ABOARD *THE DISAPPEARANCE*, SOMEWHERE IN THE SEA OF CORTEZ, 1974.

4. Donald Kuspit, "H. C. Westermann: Braving the Absurd," *Art in America* 67, no. 1 (Jan.–Feb. 1979): 85.

5. "Marine Tells How Lady Luck Rode 'Galloping Ghost,'" n.p., Westermann Papers, AAA, accessed 2024.

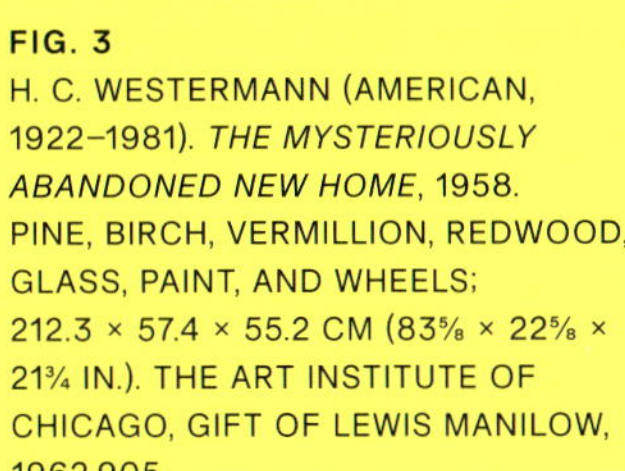

FIG. 3
H. C. WESTERMANN (AMERICAN, 1922–1981). *THE MYSTERIOUSLY ABANDONED NEW HOME*, 1958. PINE, BIRCH, VERMILLION, REDWOOD, GLASS, PAINT, AND WHEELS; 212.3 × 57.4 × 55.2 CM (83⅝ × 22⅝ × 21¾ IN.). THE ART INSTITUTE OF CHICAGO, GIFT OF LEWIS MANILOW, 1962.905.

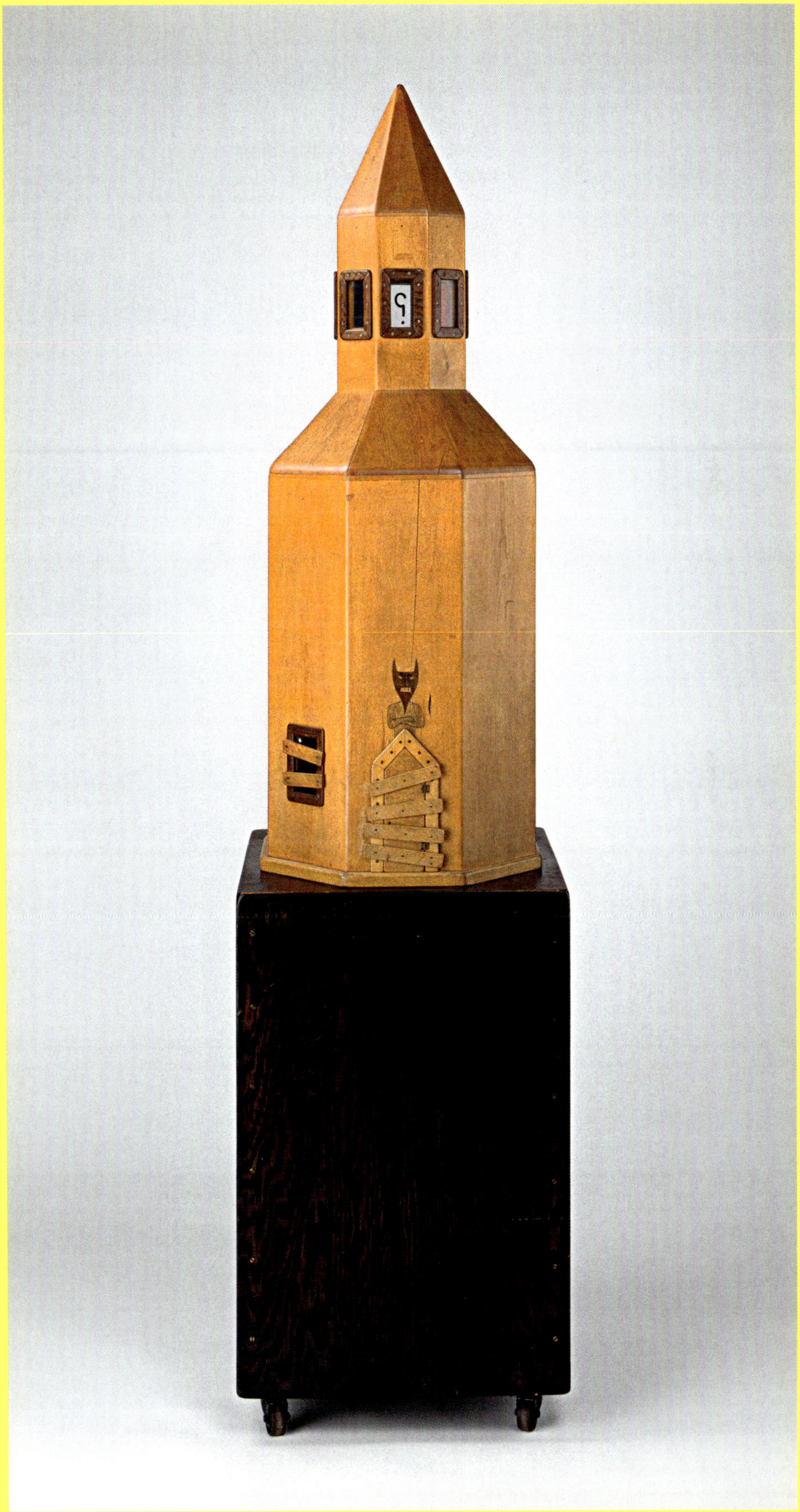

better illustrate novelist Thomas Pynchon's characterization of World War II: "The war, the absolute rule of chance."[6]

Westermann preferred not to speak about his years in the military. An article in the *Kansas City Star*, however, reveals his thoughts on how death and war were shallowly portrayed in modern culture. The artist objected to the writing of Ian Fleming, author of the James Bond novels: "Just what we need. His big contribution being to help render sex and death a little more impersonal."[7] Although Westermann's works resist straightforward biographical narrativization, they are nothing if not personal. He returned regularly to the death ship—a motif that illustrates something he saw with his own eyes. "Among his experiences," shared one newspaper profile, "[is] a gun duel with the first Kamikaze Corps plane to strike an American ship."[8] Although the *Enterprise* avoided, and survived, kamikaze attacks, Westermann watched planes successfully target the nearby USS *Franklin* and USS *Belleau Wood* during the Battle of the Philippine Sea. The artist revisited this sight twenty times in his sculptures, producing works that show the exact moment of impact as a ship is struck by a plane. *Death Ship, Out of San Pedro, Adrift* (pl. 16) is a pure distillation of this motif's physical form—ebony and soldered brass, free of assemblage and with minimal text.

War was not only a historical subject for Westermann but also a formal challenge. The scale of death and devastation that the war caused forced artists and intellectuals, among others, to question the meaning of human existence. In order to proceed as a civilization after such horrors, many had to reassess their fundamental beliefs about the human experience—and the role of art. "To write poetry after Auschwitz is barbaric," declared philosopher Theodor W. Adorno.[9] Art had to become something else if it was to function in the wake of the death camps and the atomic bomb. The strangeness of Westermann's art remains one of the most enigmatic American expressions of that change.

The artist found a compelling precedent in the 1920s and 1930s work of John Heartfield, whose pioneering political address in photomontage created a genre that remains under-recognized for its influence on twentieth- and twenty-first-century art. Whether collaging a skull onto the head of Benito Mussolini or cleverly combining text and image to mock the Nazis (see fig. 4), the

6. Thomas Pynchon, *Gravity's Rainbow* (New York: Penguin Books, 1973), 98.

7. "Art Notes," *Kansas City Star*, n.d., Westermann Papers, AAA. H. C. Westermann, originally quoted in "Letters to the Editors," *Life*, Oct. 28, 1966, 23.

8. See note 5.

9. Theodor W. Adorno, "Cultural Criticism and Society," in *Prisms* (Cambridge, MA: MIT Press, 1983), 34.

10. Ed Ruscha, letter to H. C. Westermann, Jan. 10, 1973, Westermann Papers, AAA.

DIAGNOSE

„Wodurch zog sich der Mann denn die Rückgratsverkrümmung zu?"
„Das sind die organischen Folgen des ewigen »Heil Hitler!«"
Fotomontage: John Heartfield

FIG. 4
JOHN HEARTFIELD (GERMAN, 1891–
1968). *UNTITLED (DIAGNOSIS)*, 1935.
PHOTOGRAVURE OF PHOTOMONTAGE
BY HEARTFIELD; 37.9 × 27 CM
(14¹⁵⁄₁₆ × 10⅝⁄₁₆ IN.) THE ART INSTITUTE
OF CHICAGO, D. WENDELL FENTRESS
MEMORIAL FUND, 1993.358.

German artist developed an apt technique to address the disjunction of the contemporary conflict. Westermann eventually sent a book of photomontage to Ruscha, a friend with whom he shared, above all, a love of conceptual word-play and the finely made. In a 1973 letter, Ruscha thanked Westermann for the gift: "The John Heartfield book came at a time when nothing else would have done better."[10]

Westermann's and Ruscha's interest in Heartfield illuminates another shared characteristic of their work: the synthesis of the handmade and the assembled. Although Westermann's precise forms and construction methods stand in contrast to the junky materials and scrappy presentation associated with assemblage, one of his sculptures appeared in William C. Seitz's 1961 *Art of Assemblage* exhibition at the Museum of Modern Art, New York (MoMA), one of the most important historical showcases of the technique. Unlike some of the notable artists represented in that exhibition—like Robert Rauschenberg, Joseph Cornell, and Bruce Conner—Westermann created primarily handcrafted objects. Sometimes he assembled them into environments or constructions reminiscent of dioramas, calling to mind the found object without being found objects. For example, *Rotting Jet Wing* (pl. 8), one of the artist's many shadow boxes, holds what the title suggests is the broken wing of a fighter jet. Despite being finely made in pine, the work looks like a found fragment, largely because of its contextualization; the encased object resembles a museological display. At the same time, *Rotting Jet Wing* most recalls a specific object, as defined by Donald Judd: a singular object that cannot be broken down into its constituent parts. In Westermann's sculpture, the mode of display forms an inextricable part of the work, not a trick. Similarly, Heartfield's works are not intended to confuse reality or circulate as manipulations of truth. Instead, both artists foregrounded their artifice—with great skill—in order to make their art, and in so doing, foregrounded the coexistence of the handmade and the assembled. And like Heartfield, Westermann developed this approach as a result of making art in the wake of war.

It was precisely this combination of the handmade and the assembled, the overlap between the rendered and the readymade, and the simultaneity of the crafted and the conceptual that made Westermann's work so influential. Tellingly, his work appeared in a trilogy of exhibitions that set the stage for American art of the 1960s. In addition to being in the previously mentioned *Art of Assemblage*, Westermann's art also featured in Peter Selz's *New Images of Man* (1959) and William S. Rubin's *Dada, Surrealism, and Their Heritage* (1968), all at MoMA. Westermann's inclusion in these exhibitions attests not to a similarity in their theses, which were in fact somewhat distinct across art historical, philosophical, and formal lines, but it does speak to the singularity of his art. Critical discourses had not yet ossified into the categories of Pop, Minimalism, and Conceptual Art—categories that came to characterize later art historical periodization but struggled to encapsulate Westermann's work—and there was still room for assemblage, Funk, Neo-Dada, and other approaches to contend within the soup of the present. That Westermann, unlike other artists, moved easily between these categories is reflected by the peculiar admiration bestowed upon him—despite his lack of mainstream recognition—by such widely differing artists as Judd and the Chicago Imagists.

Take, for example, certain 1960s works by Bruce Nauman. It is well documented that in 1965, while students at the University of California, Davis, Nauman and William T. Wiley began a brief correspondence with Westermann. They eventually met at artist Peter Saul's studio, and while Wiley and Westermann remained friends, it seems Nauman and Westermann did not continue any kind of relationship. Yet Nauman made a sculpture in 1967 that directly references Westermann's work. *Westermann's Ear* (fig. 5), part of a series focused on knots, consists of a plaster ear attached to a length of rope and does not represent Westermann any more than Nauman's *Henry Moore Bound to Fail (Back View)* (1967–70; Saint Louis Art Museum) illustrates Moore's back. As art historian Jo Applin has noted, Nauman's choice

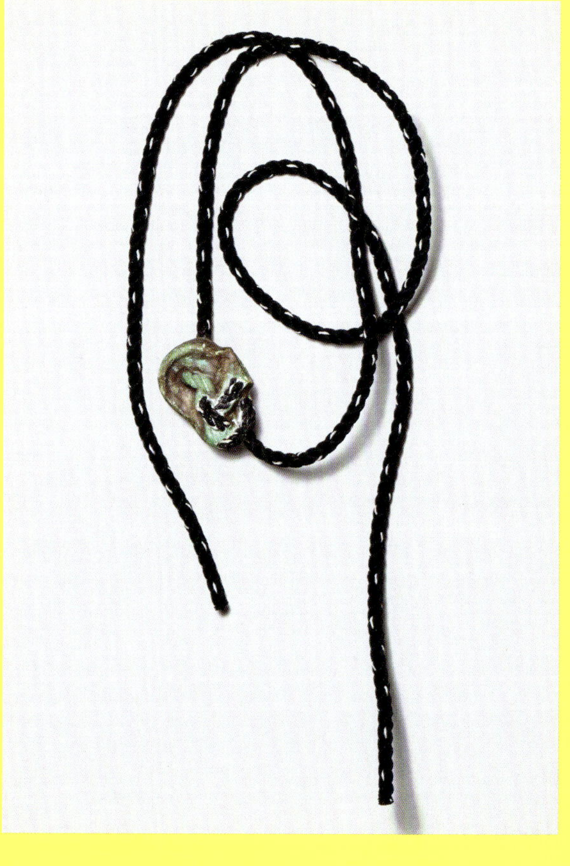

11. Jo Applin, "Hauntings: Bruce Nauman," in *Eccentric Objects: Rethinking Sculpture in 1960s America* (New Haven, CT: Yale University Press, 2012), aaeportal.com/?id=-15447.

12. Donald Judd, "Local History," *Arts Yearbook 7*, 1964. For the quotation, see Max Kozloff, *H. C. Westermann*, exh. cat. (Los Angeles: Los Angeles County Museum of Art, 1968), 7.

13. H. C. Westermann, letter to Allan Frumkin, Feb. 17, 1965, in *Letters from H. C. Westermann*, ed. Bill Barrette (New York: Timken Publishers, 1988), 60. His focus on, and affection for, all things American comes through in his work as well; the title of *Little Egypt* (pl. 12), for example, might have been inspired by an eponymous region of southern Illinois, which earned its nickname in the nineteenth century for its excess of farmland and stereotypical vacancy.

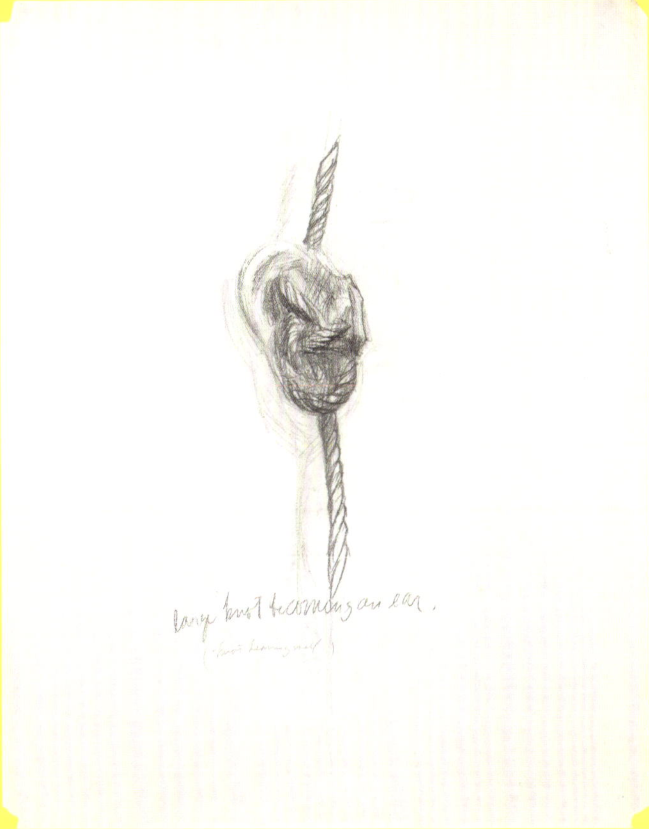

of artists for these works was strange: "By 1966 both Westermann's and Moore's works had been all but excluded from contemporary discourse on art. Westermann…occupied an awkward, marginal position in the art scene, while Moore, although a member of the 'most visible generation of British Modernists' of the 1930s, by the mid-sixties was such a familiar figure that he was to all intents and purposes invisible to the younger generation of post-war sculptors."[11] The same year he made *Westermann's Ear*, Nauman drew *Large Knot Becoming an Ear (Knot Hearing Well)* (fig. 6). The illustrated rope is tied in a large, complex knot in the middle that is highly reminiscent of Westermann's 1963 sculpture *The Big Change* (pl. 3), one of three large laminated plywood pieces critic Dennis Adrian discussed in his in-depth *Artforum* cover story on the artist's work in September of 1967, the year Nauman created his homages.

Some analyses suggest that these Moore- and Westermann-inspired pieces express the anxiety of influence, the steps taken by a young artist to forge his own path. Yet the knot—as it bounces from *The Big Change* to Nauman's drawing and then to *Westermann's Ear*—illuminates one of the qualities of Westermann's sculptures that fixated artists in the 1960s. Nauman's fascination with Westermann's knots, just like Judd's christening of Westermann's art in his category of specific objects as early as 1964, reflects the desire of artists in the 1960s to make objects for which "one does not know which one of several conceivable interpretations most applies."[12]

These qualities of Westermann's work—and his influence—would not escape international attention, despite the artist's own objection. "I am an American artist + don't give one God damn about the international scene (which is pretty weak in general)," he wrote to his dealer Allan Frumkin in 1965.[13] As a result of this attitude, Westermann appears not to have traveled internationally after the Korean War. The irony is that Westermann's Americanness became not a sign of provincialism but instead a quality that, in the 1960s and 1970s, appealed to the international exhibition circuit, and his works appeared in many major exhibitions of the 1970s.

FIG. 6
NAUMAN. *LARGE KNOT BECOMING AN EAR (KNOT HEARING WELL)*, 1967. PENCIL; 86.7 × 69 CM (34 × 27 IN.). KUNSTMUSEUM BASEL.

When Swiss curator Harald Szeemann visited Chicago to prepare for Documenta 5, in Kassel, Germany, he encountered Westermann's work not only in the home of Art Institute of Chicago Director A. James Speyer but also on display at the museum itself (see fig. 7). During his research trip, Szeemann may have heard more about the artist's works from friends of Westermann he met, including Ruscha (who would design the Documenta 5 catalogue) and Wiley, among others. As a result, Westermann appeared in Documenta 5 with his sculpture *Little Egypt* (see fig. 8; pl. 12). Predictably, he did not travel to Kassel, but his dealer visited the exhibition and reported back. "*Little Egypt* is doing fine," wrote Frumkin, "Taking some slamming but it is bearing it well—good construction wins out! (and the key + doorknob are shiny from use)."[14]

Documenta 5 showcased a range of artists—such as Daniel Buren, Gerhard Richter, Hans Haacke, and Blinky Palermo, as well as Ruscha, Wiley, and Nauman—whose works would redefine what constitutes a work of art for decades to come.[15] It also, as Benjamin Buchloh noted, "opened the exhibition to a notion of visual culture that threw into the sharpest possible relief the obsolescent isolation of autonomous high culture."[16] Westermann's inclusion attests to the enigmatic importance of his sculpture at the time, where it fit quite perfectly alongside works by Hermann Nitsch, Sigmar Polke, and Lucas Samaras, as well as Cornell, in whose proximity Westermann's sculpture was installed. Unlike the cool conceptualism championed elsewhere in the exhibition, these artists sought ways to make art in the present that emerged from their own personal mythologies.

The following year, Westermann was represented in the 12th São Paulo Biennial (1973) alongside a group of twelve artists

14. Allan Frumkin, letter to H. C. Westermann, May 27, 1977, Westermann Papers, AAA.

15. Not nearly enough can be said about the influence of Documenta 5 or the cross section of artists it represented.

16. Benjamin H. D. Buchloh, "Documenta 7: A Dictionary of Received Ideas," *October* 22 (Autumn 1982): 105–26, doi .org/10.2307/778366.

17. The United States' participation in previous São Paulo Biennials was marred by artists dropping out in protest of the Brazilian military regime at the time and a lack of funding; as a result, this unofficial participation was overseen by Walter Hopps and Donald Baum. David L. Shirey, "12 U.S. Artists, First Since '67, Chosen for the Sao Paulo Bienal [*sic*]," *New York Times*, May 24, 1973, 53, timesmachine.nytimes.com /timesmachine/1973/05/24/99146639 .html?pageNumber=53.

18. "Sao Paulo Biennial Is Stalked by Controversy," *New York Times*, Dec. 26, 1973, 56, timesmachine.nytimes.com /timesmachine/1973/12/26/80818354 .html?pageNumber=56.

19. Isobel Whitelegg, "How to Talk About Biennials That Don't Exist: Reassembling the Twelfth São Paulo Biennial (1973)," *Tate Papers*, no. 34 (2021–22): tate.org.uk /research/tate-papers/34/biennials-that -dont-exist-reassembling-twelfth-sao-paulo -biennial-1973.

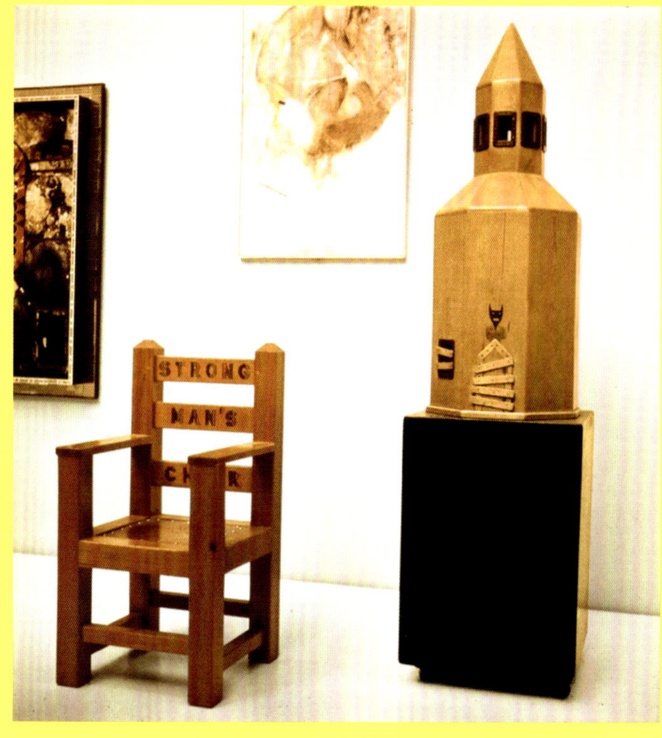

FIG. 7
INSTALLATION VIEW OF *THE MYSTERIOUSLY ABANDONED NEW HOME*, THE ART INSTITUTE OF CHICAGO, 1971.

During his visit to Chicago, Szeemann saw this installation by Speyer featuring works by Westermann, Jess Collins, and Bruce Conner.

associated with the city of Chicago, including Jim Nutt and Gladys Nilsson, as well as other Chicago Imagists. At the time, the *New York Times* reported that it was unknown whether or not the American artists would be able to compete for prizes, due to their unofficial status in the biennial.[17] Yet Westermann himself would win a cash prize at the exhibition.[18] Just as Documenta 5 marked a major achievement for international conceptual art in Europe, the 12th São Paulo Biennial displayed radical new artistic production from the nation, so much so that it was met with outright hostility by conservative factions of the Brazilian art scene.[19]

THE WORK EXHIBITED IN DOCUMENTA 5—*LITTLE EGYPT*—EXEMPLIFIES Westermann's approach to sculpture. On a well-proportioned base sits a door. A bit smaller than one would expect, the door is nonetheless fully operational, with a knob, a working lock, and a key that cannot be removed. Made entirely by hand, like all of his works—as well as his home and studio in Connecticut—the sculpture is held together with bolts and hinges that Westermann created himself (and stamped *HCW*). Although a note carved across the top of the frame informs us that the door *should* always be closed (see p. 86), the work *can* be opened—and as Frumkin shared from Kassel, it was regularly handled while on display. *Little Egypt*, however, is a portal to nowhere, a door to nothing—a culmination of Westermann's perfect exteriors hiding interiors that, even when accessed, prove empty. This quality made his work a touchstone for so many artists of the 1960s and 1970s who pursued new forms of oblique expression and sought to make well-crafted works that avoided the pitfalls of meaning and interpretation, which had come to plague Abstract Expressionism by the 1950s. For Westermann, these empty, inaccessible interiors allowed him to exorcise the atrocities of war from his psyche. To make a perfect box that can hold one's terrors—and to empty it symbolically—encapsulates the psychology of a generation. ⚓

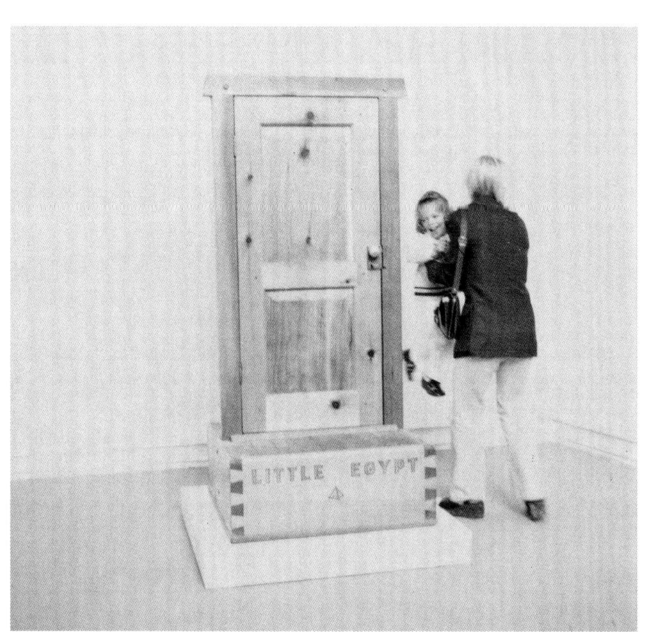

FIG. 8
INSTALLATION VIEW OF *LITTLE EGYPT*, DOCUMENTA 5, KASSEL, GERMANY, JUNE 30–OCT. 8, 1972.

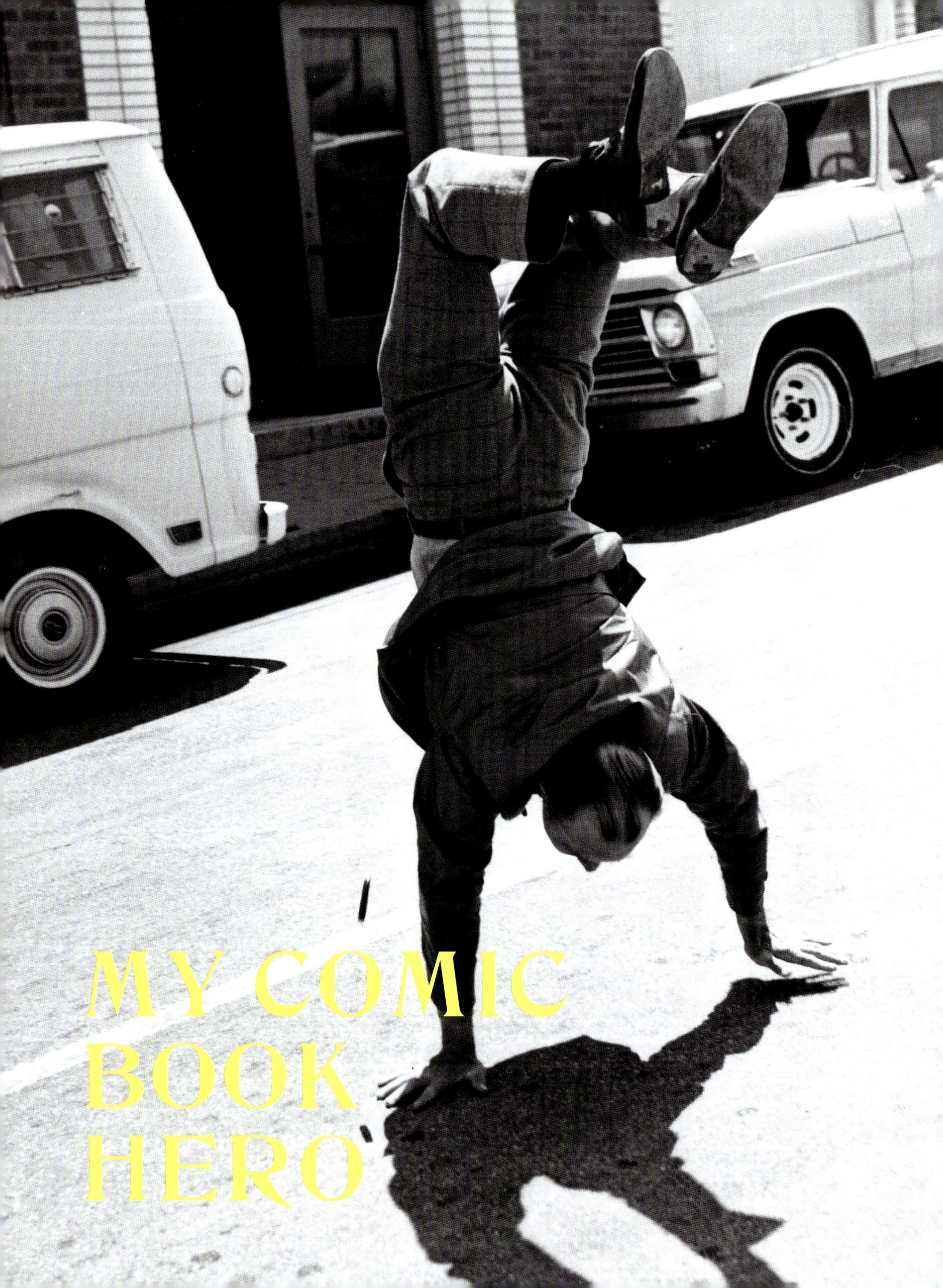

MY COMIC
BOOK
HERO

ED RUSCHA
WITH
GIAMPAOLO BIANCONI

This interview was conducted on May 15, 2024. The text has been edited for length and clarity.

Giampaolo Bianconi (GB)   How did you first meet H. C. Westermann?

Ed Ruscha (ER)   He was at the Tamarind Lithography Workshop in Los Angeles, working on *See America First*, a print portfolio that he made.

GB   Did you spend time with him while he was working?

ER   Not while he was working there, but I would see him socially. He seemed to connect with all these people out there, namely Billy Al Bengston and Larry Bell, and other artists—Tony Berlant, Ken Price, who was also a good friend of his, and Ed Moses. Those people seemed to entertain him when he came to town, and he liked them a lot. So I was around for a lot of that, and I got to know him.

Right away I could see that Cliff was a genuine American character. I always thought he was like a cross between Popeye and Dick Tracy. It's kind of indescribable, except that he was a skyscraper of an artist. You have to stand back and love his life and everything about it. He was a dynamic character without ever pretending to be, because he was modest in a lot of his behavior.

It was a joy to be around him. He was a tough guy with a heart of gold. People like that exist. But he had lots of other sides to him, mainly related to his history. We learned right away that he was in World War II and he was on an aircraft carrier, the USS *Enterprise*. He saw some horrific things in the Pacific theater fighting against the Japanese. He watched sister ships get bombed and go down. He talked about his experiences, and wrote about them, and made drawings of them, and it infiltrated his art. The dark thoughts that come out of wartime—sinking ships and rats—those are all there.

GB   He had a sharp wit that you see not only in the titles of his works but also in the works themselves, which have a lot of writing on them. And he had a way with words that was enigmatic.

ER   Everything that came my way by him was a surprise. He was always making an effort to tell his story: the war, and going off to battle, and all those experiences shadowed him as a dark history. So the wit and the wordplay might seem mysterious, but they have a connection to his life.

GB   But he had a playful side that was physical, too.

ER   He was a gymnast, swimmer, and diver (see fig. 1). And he did handstands. He loved to walk on his hands. And whenever he did that, he would make sure his pockets were full of coins, so they'd all roll out all over the floor. It was like a theater piece, but he was just doing it for the fun of it.

FIG. 1
H. C. WESTERMANN AND BILLY AL BENGSTON DIVING, 1960s.

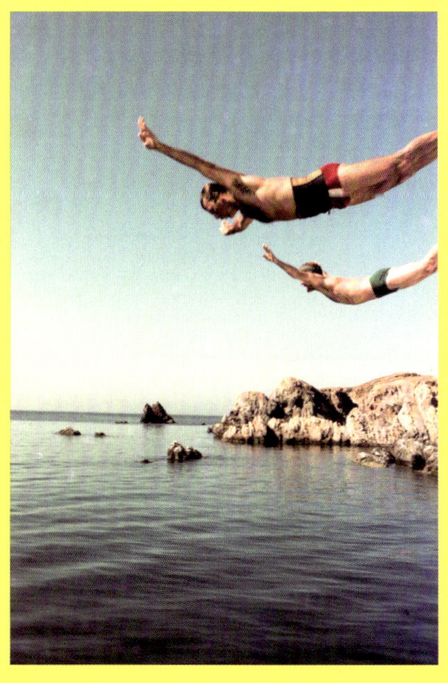

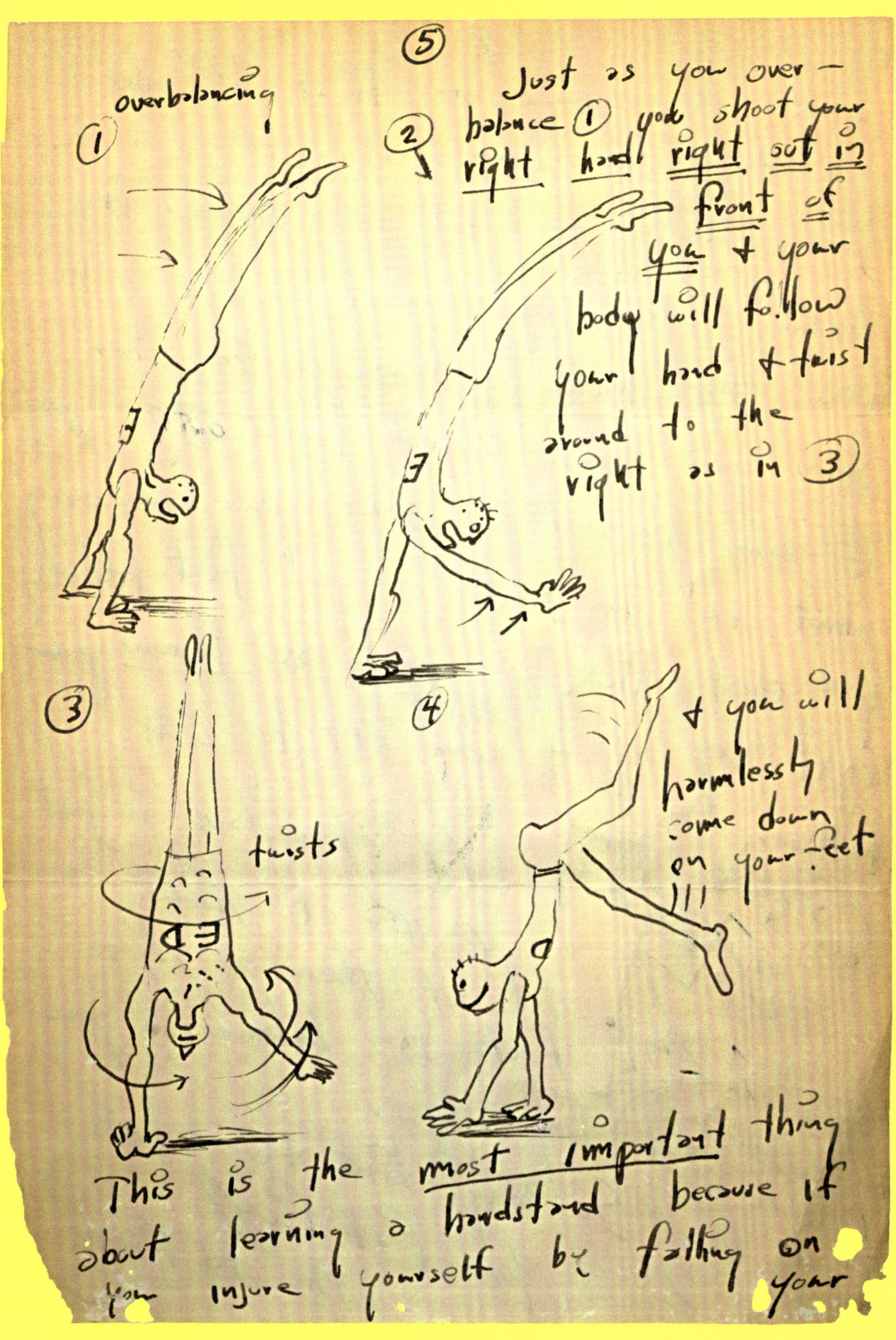
overbalancing
①
⑤
② Just as you over—
balance ① you shoot your
right hand right out in
front of
you & your
body will follow
your hand & twist
around to the
right as in ③
③
twists
④
& you will
harmlessly
come down
on your feet
This is the most important thing
about learning a handstand because if
you injure yourself by falling on your

One time, I said to him, "Boy, that handstand you do, that's pretty good. How do you do that anyway?" And he said, "Well, I'll tell you sometime." Then later I get a letter (fig. 2) in the mail with drawings of four, five easy steps to doing a handstand, and showing how when you overbalance, you just whip your hand around and won't hurt yourself. I was always too scared to try it.

GB I know you kept in touch by mail—did you ever visit?

ER Over the years I visited him twice at his place in Brookfield, Connecticut. The first time he was living in a nice house off in the country that was owned by his father-in-law, Lester Beall, who was a respected industrial designer. Cliff married his daughter, Joanna, who also was an artist. I've got a watercolor or two by her. He would call Joanna "the little woman" and had nothing but love for her. They had a great life together.

In Brookfield I remember he had a tiny, one-room studio. And his two walls were taken up with painted silhouettes of tools. Where there's the silhouette of a hammer on the wall, you put a hammer on that silhouette.

That's the way Cliff lived. And he loved making things, loved woodworking, loved metalworking, anything like that.

GB How did you relate to his work before you met him?

ER His work was not trendy by any sense of the word. He didn't come out of the Abstract Expressionist mode, but he was probably affected by it. And he had a wide-ranging interest in all forms of art. There was something like folk art about it in a way, but informed by the world of art and the history of art.

His work came down to folk art in the sense that it was handcrafted and made by the artist, hands on. He was a true artist with hands on the job, and he would be at a loss to hire other people to fabricate things for him. He made everything himself. He'd talk about it, too. So he would say, "I go to a hardware store in Connecticut, and they have cheap tools that come from Asia, and I don't like them. I make my own tools. I make my own bolts and nuts." He would do that. He would make them out of bronze, and heavy metals, and things like that. He didn't have a metalworking shop with lathes, I don't think, but he made do with simple things. He loved crafting by hand, and all his things are easily recognized as being lovingly made by hand.

And then the sort of lyrical poetry behind these works, you could see that he had a particular slant on life, and it would filter right down into the very works that he was making. I've got a dustpan that he made out of galvanized metal. He made many of them (see fig. 3), and he would give

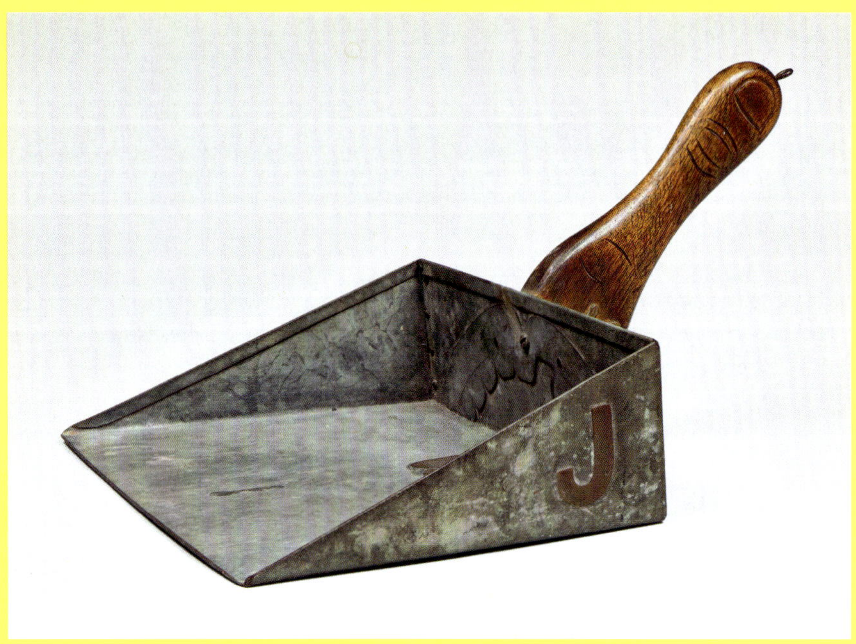

them out and say, "Now, God damn, Ed, I want you to use those. I want you to use that thing. Don't just put it up on the mantle and look at it like a work of art. Use it." He was always talking that way, and I think he meant it, too. He wanted people to appreciate his art, but he also wanted you to get some fundamental use out of these things.

Billy Al Bengston loved Cliff, and he said, "Cliff makes about fifty gifts every year, and about five works of art." He made things for people all the time.

GB A lot of artists looked up to him.

ER I think that most artists were surprised to see Cliff as someone who was there but not a part of a swinging moment that was happening in the forward motion of art. They viewed him, and I do too, as somebody particularly unique. He didn't really care much about the hot artists at the time. He was different than them. People valued his stance because he didn't participate in the ongoing trajectory of art. He was outside of it in his own peculiar way.

GB There was a lot of healthy skepticism then, as there is now, toward museums and the art world. He felt that, too.

ER He did—but he did play the art game. He had art dealers, Allan Frumkin and Rolf Nelson, and he knew how to work with them and he didn't always like it. He wasn't an outsider who didn't participate in the commercial art world; he sold his work. I think he liked his dealers but was skeptical of their aims. And I think he had a built-in skepticism of the commerce of art, of course he did, but at the same time, he would participate in it, and he would deal with museums and galleries. But he didn't have a studio full of people helping him.

GB You mentioned you visited him twice?

ER The second time, I saw the studio he built. He was still working on it, too—I think he was maybe always working on it. Everything in that studio was overbuilt. If something was usually 4 by 4, he made it 8 by 8. I think he had a disdain for the way people were doing things, the way carpenters and machinists were trying to cut corners, and he didn't want to cut corners. He wanted to make things solid and permanent. That was his voice there.

GB He was a real hands-on guy—do you think that was different from ideas that were circulating around Los Angeles when you encountered him?

ER Yeah. All the artists were into materials, and that was good to see—people working in plastics, light, and paint, of course. But working with all these materials, it would seem to be an indulgence in materials for all the artists, especially to Cliff. He was into the bare bones of carpentry and joinery and fitting things together.

GB I've noticed that a lot of the sculptures from Alan and Dorothy Press include little compartments or secret areas where Westermann listed all of the materials that are in the sculpture, and also some of the details about how he made them. It's almost as if you're remodeling a house and you take down a wall and find someone left a note in there describing what was going on a hundred years ago when they were building the house. There's something very emotional about that.

ER I know it. And you see it in his work. You really see it.

When my son was about one year old, Cliff made him a little rocking horse out of some wood and a cut-off piece of a tree that was shaped like a horse, with a horse's mouth and everything. And then the rocker part of it was very well-made. I think he steamed the wood to curve it. He got really into it. And not only that, he would use intaglio stamps that he would pound into wood to say "red oak" or "coal," the materials he used. He called them out on the works. They were almost instructional.

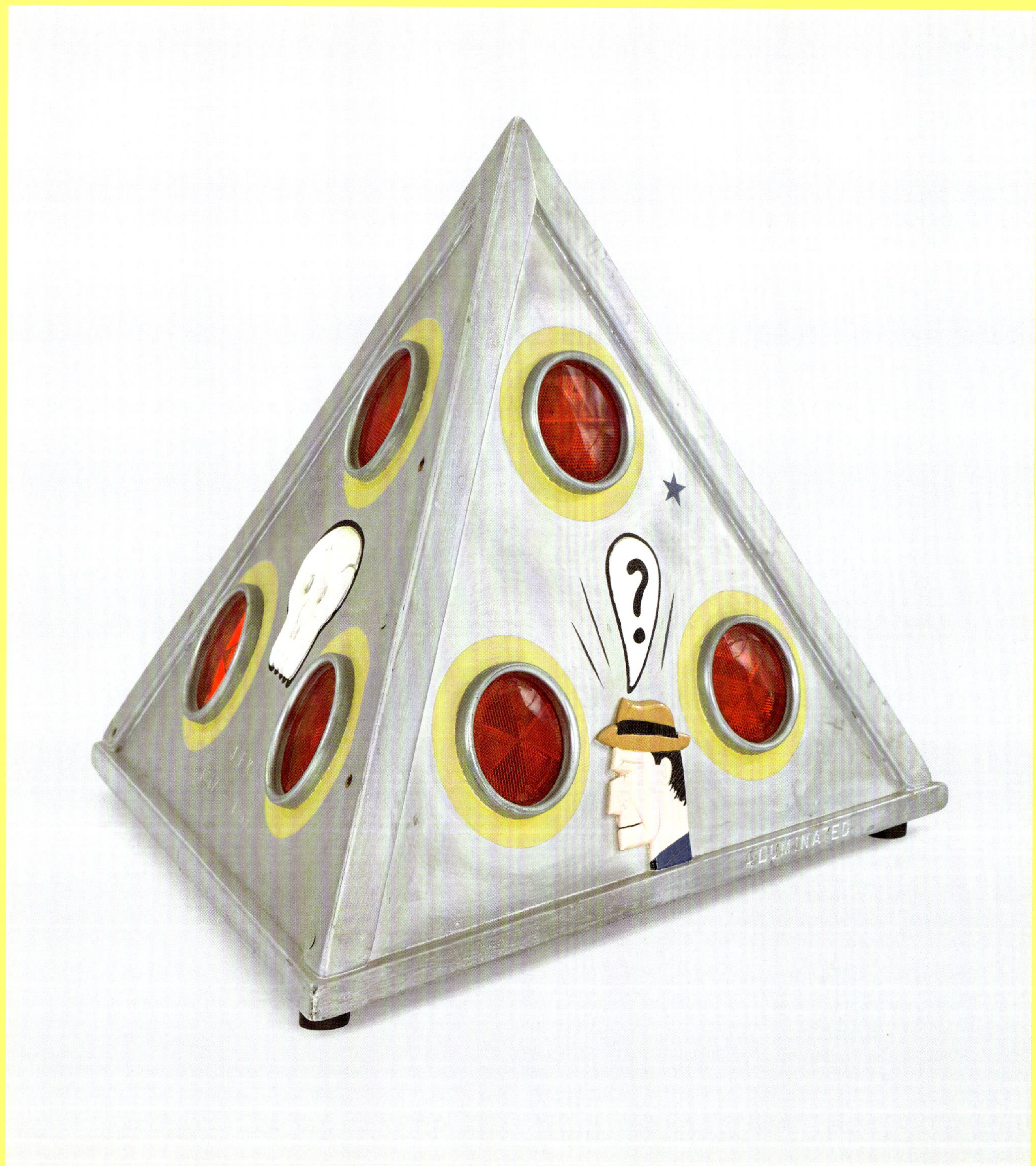
ILLUMINATED

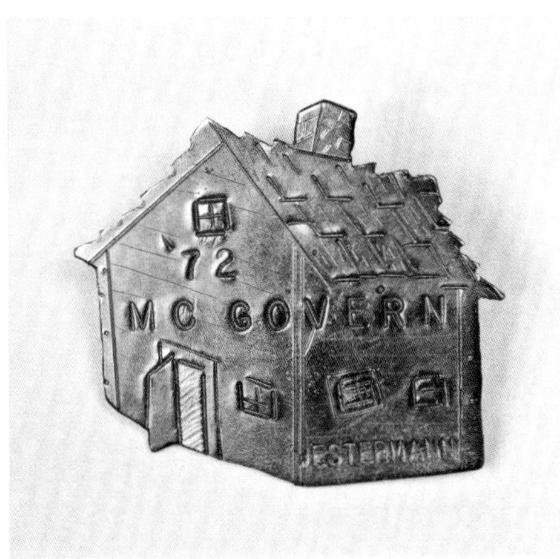

FIG. 4

WESTERMANN. *UNTITLED (MCGOVERN PIN–LOG CABIN)*, 1972. BRASS; 5.1 × 5.7 CM (2 × 2¼ IN.). THE SMART MUSEUM OF ART, THE H. C. WESTERMANN STUDY COLLECTION, GIFT OF THE ESTATE OF JOANNA BEALL WESTERMANN.

South Dakota Senator George McGovern ran his 1972 presidential campaign on an anti-war platform. He lost the election to Richard Nixon.

FIG. 5

WESTERMANN. *ALUMINATED*, 1964. MARINE PLYWOOD, MASONITE, ALUMINUM, ALKYD ENAMEL, REFLECTORS, ENAMEL, MIRROR, AND RUBBER BUMPERS; 48 × 55 × 56 CM (18⅞ × 21⅝ × 22⁄₁₆ IN.). COLLECTION OF JIM NEWMAN AND JANE IVORY.

GB Speaking of gifts—I read that he once gave you a book by John Heartfield. I thought that was an interesting choice. There's a lot about Westermann's work that comes out of Heartfield in a way. I can see that he would relate to those anti-authoritarian sentiments (see fig. 4) and caricatures in a big way.

ER Oh, yeah. He liked Heartfield. I vaguely knew about him—he was part of art history study, Dada and Germany and fascism (see p. 15, fig. 4). I wasn't quite sure what I thought about him, and I guess Cliff knew about that and sent me this book, which I've got on my lap right now. He just thought I would respond to it, and I did.

He sent me another book. You know *Fat City*?

GB The one John Huston made into a movie?

ER Yeah, Leonard Gardner's *Fat City*. He sent me this book in 1974. He liked to write things out, and he said, "Dear Ed, thanks for that funny duck." I don't know what he was talking about. Maybe I sent him a duck. "It was swell seeing you again and your fine work. Hope you enjoy this book as I did. We had a great time in Mexico and didn't get sick until we hit that lousy Tucson. Sincerely Cliff. Say hello to Pauly"—he called my brother Paul, Pauly—and then that anchor, that little anchor. His signature.

GB Why do you think he was so generous with his gifts?

ER I don't know, but I think it was all about art, even the gifts.

He had a dream one time that I was in the desert, and I had a house with a spiral staircase. I was going up this staircase, and it had a string for a railing. Cliff was there with me and he said, "Ed, you're going to bust your ass. That string is not going to hold." And he said, "Now, and also, you need some varnish for those steps." So he sent me this box, which was very beautifully made, a box that held three cans of marine varnish. And then that box goes inside of a crate that Cliff made by himself. And you can see the time that he spent on this shipping crate. It was all an artwork to him.

He spent his time loving what he did, and that was that. That's what made him my comic book hero (see fig. 5). ⚓

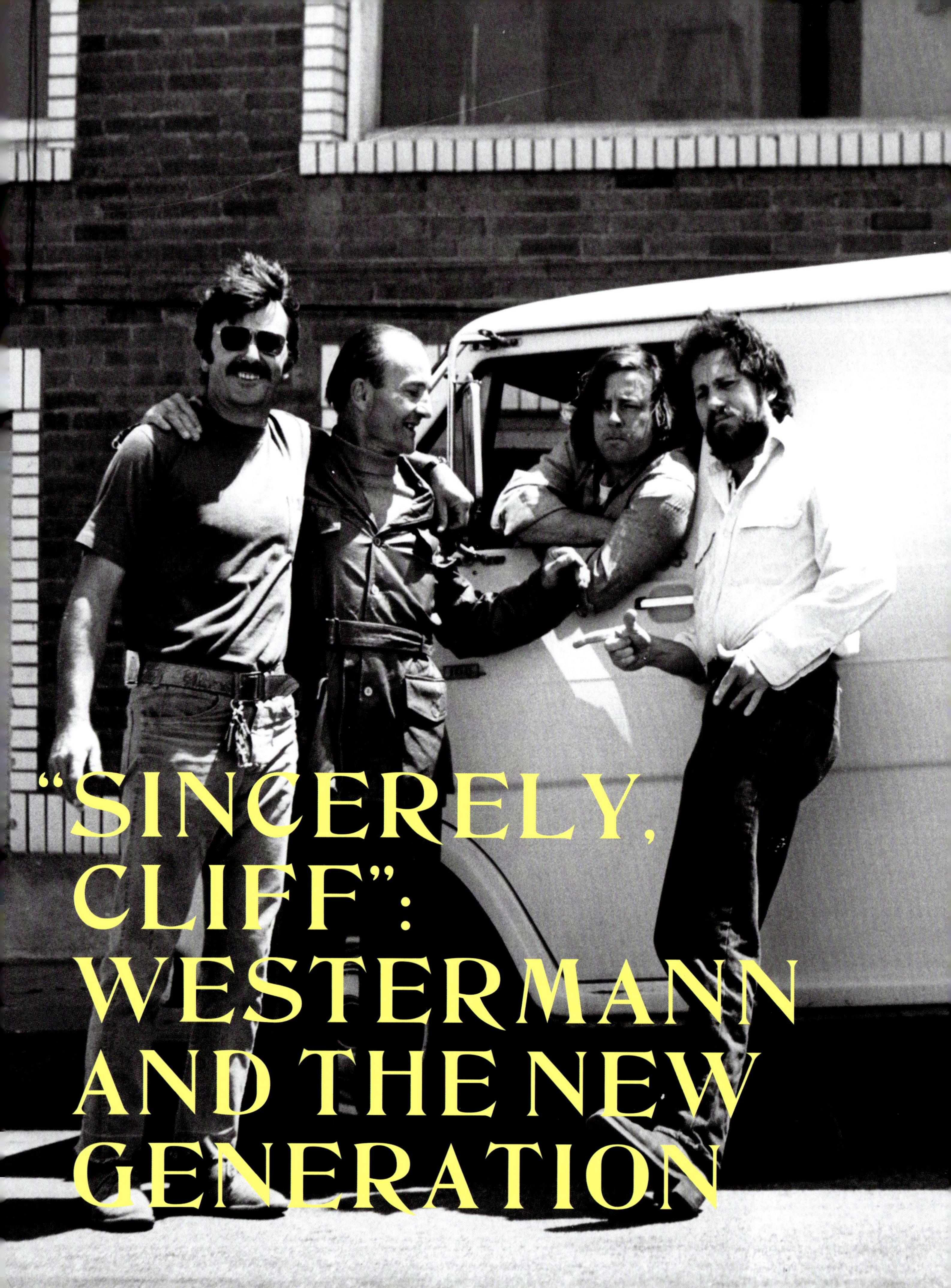

"SINCERELY,
CLIFF":
WESTERMANN
AND THE NEW
GENERATION

THEA LIBERTY NICHOLS

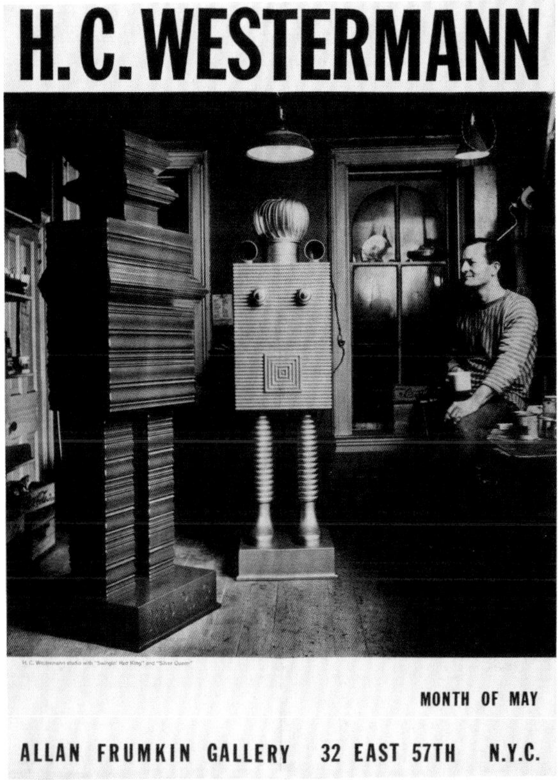

FIG. 1
H. C. WESTERMANN (AMERICAN, 1922–1981). EXHIBITION POSTER FOR *H. C. WESTERMANN*, 1961. OFFSET LITHOGRAPH ON PAPER; SHEET: 56 × 40.5 CM (22⅟₁₆ × 16 IN.). THE ART INSTITUTE OF CHICAGO, GIFT OF GLADYS NILSSON AND JIM NUTT, 2018.22.

H. C. WESTERMANN WAS "ADMIRED ACROSS THE AESTHETIC spectrum" by artists during his lifetime.[1] He also enjoyed success from the outset of his career: his early sculptures—death ships and dollhouse-like boxes reminiscent of Mexican retables—attracted the support of a who's who of mid-century Chicago's most important and influential curatorial, cultural, and commercial voices. Among them were art historian and critic Katharine Kuh, who tried valiantly to bring *The Evil New War God (S.O.B.)* (1958; Whitney Museum of American Art) into the Art Institute of Chicago's collection; acclaimed architect Ludwig Mies van der Rohe, Westermann's first patron, who purchased *Butterfly* (1957; Collection of Dirk Lohan, Chicago) the year it was made; and gallerist Allan Frumkin, who would represent the artist in Chicago and New York for the majority of the artist's career (see fig. 1).

Westermann's success in Chicago led to greater visibility of his artwork in California, first in solo exhibitions at the Dilexi Gallery's Los Angeles location in 1962 and its San Francisco venue in 1963 (both of which originated at Frumkin's Chicago and New York galleries, respectively). These shows put his work in front of artists up and down the California coast, and his inclusion in *American Sculptors of the Sixties*, held at the Los Angeles County Museum of Art in 1967, positioned him as a forebearer of Funk Art. His introduction on the West Coast mirrored that in Chicago: many young Chicagoans first encountered Westermann's work in solo exhibitions held at Allan Frumkin Gallery, and his inclusion in the seminal *Made in Chicago*, organized by the Museum of Contemporary Art Chicago in 1975, recognized his foundational role in the development of Chicago Imagism (often seen as a corollary to Funk Art).[2]

Westermann's powerful reception belies the fact that he sought to engage the art world selectively and on his own terms, preferring to focus on the labor of his craft instead—a decision cemented by his move to Brookfield, Connecticut, in 1961 with his new wife, artist Joanna Beall. While working primarily at a remove from this young vanguard of artists in Chicago and California

1. Sarah Canright, phone call with the author, Dec. 1, 2023.

2. In addition to exhibiting in many other major museum and gallery exhibitions, H. C. Westermann showed work alongside both California and Chicago artists in a touring version of *Human Concern/Personal Torment*, held at University of California, Berkley, in 1970. Westermann's work also featured in the landmark 1972 exhibition *Chicago Imagist Art*, held at the Museum of Contemporary Art Chicago, and in group shows over two decades at the Renaissance Society at the University of Chicago (a bellwether of contemporary art locally and nationally), appearing alongside a wide range of artists associated with Chicago Imagism, Conceptual Art, Dada, and Minimalism.

throughout the 1960s and 1970s, Westermann remained in conversation and, at times, in direct contact with them, his artwork often preceding and, in some cases, standing in for him. Over time he developed relationships with many of these artists based on mutual admiration and respect for each other's work—not dictated by style or theme, which varied greatly among them, but rather linked by spirit: they emerged from similar traditions, including a pervasive Surrealist sensibility in both regions, yet rejected the labels applied to them and the artistic precedent they inherited, such as the dominance of figurative painting by the artists of Bay Area Figuration and Chicago's Monster Roster.[3] As Northern California sculptor David King described, "Westermann loved many artists…respected their unique ideas, their passion for quality, and their offbeat perspective on society."[4]

Westermann, in turn, made an impression on this younger generation through his strength of character, which stemmed from a spirited individualism and hard-earned anti-militarism.[5] The Los Angeles native left home at age nineteen and gained spectacularly varied professional experience as an acrobat, railroad repairman, and US Marine before moving to Chicago to enroll in the applied arts program at the School of the Art Institute of Chicago (SAIC) under the G. I. Bill of Rights. Interrupting his studies to reenlist and serve in the Korean War from 1951 to 1952, he reenrolled in SAIC's fine art program upon his disillusioned return and graduated in 1954 at a mature thirty-two. The independence Westermann modeled in his life and in his art making greatly encouraged young emerging Chicago artists; resonated with the free-spirited, countercultural, and anti-establishment politics of the New Left fomenting in the Bay Area; and illustrated the fluidity between art and life, which proved relevant to the more cerebral expressions of artists emerging in Southern California. The

3. The exhibition program at the San Francisco Museum of Modern Art was largely responsible for the Surrealist sensibility in the Bay Area as early as the interwar period, and the Allan Frumkin Gallery was "instrumental in introducing the European Surrealists" to Chicago at midcentury. Roberta Smith, "Allan Frumkin, Art Dealer in Two Cities, Is Dead at 75," *New York Times*, Dec. 12, 2002, section B, page 11, nytimes.com/2002/12/12/arts/allan-frumkin-art-dealer-in-two-cities-is-dead-at-75.html. Other Chicago artists gained limited exposure in Northern California during this period in exhibitions such as *Hairy Who?*, San Francisco Art Institute (SFAI), May 3–29, 1968; *Famous Artists from Chicago*, Sacramento State College, Mar. 10–24, 1970; and *Surplus Slop from the Windy City*, SFAI, Apr. 16–May 16, 1970. The work of Jim Nutt and Gladys Nilsson was featured at the Candy Store Gallery in Folsom, California, and Nutt, Nilsson, and later Karl Wirsum were hired by Sacramento State College (now University) as instructors in the early 1970s. For an incisive outline of the overlap between Chicago and California artists in the 1960s, see Whitney Chadwick, "Narrative Imagism and the Figurative Tradition in Northern California Painting," *Art Journal* 45, no. 4 (Winter 1985): 310.

4. David King, *H. C. Westermann: West* (Richmond, CA: Richmond Art Center, 1997), 31.

5. For more on Westermann's military experiences before embarking on a career as an artist, see pages 12–14 in this volume.

6. For more on Westermann's international reception, see pages 17–19 in this volume.

7. Westermann even confessed in an illustrated letter to Chicago artists Ed Flood and Sarah Canright that "every time I make a drawing it's a self-portrait." Quoted in Bill Barrette, ed., *Letters from H. C. Westermann* (New York: Timken Publishers, 1988), 121.

breadth of Westermann's appeal among artists, curators, and collectors in the Midwest, on the West Coast, and abroad points to the permeability of modern art movements in the making and the links between him and myriad artists and movements of the postwar period.[6]

DURING HIS EARLY YEARS IN CHICAGO, WESTERMANN EXHIBITED IN A number of Art Institute annuals and in the Art Institute counter-salon *Exhibition Momentum* (1956 and 1957), but it was *New Images of Man* (1959) at the Museum of Modern Art, New York—featuring three Westermann sculptures alongside work by Cosmo Campoli and Leon Golub—that led to his affiliation with the Monster Roster. The term was coined in 1959 to describe a group of Chicago-based artists, including Westermann, Campoli, Golub, June Leaf, and Nancy Spero, whose expressionistic figuration challenged the then-dominant Abstract Expressionist movement.

Despite critics grouping Westermann with these artists, his work stood in stark contrast to theirs—especially Golub's, the group's unofficial figurehead. Both artists were veterans and SAIC alumnus with a shared interest in war-related subject matter, but Golub produced monumental unstretched canvases of classical and heroic figures in existential crisis, their mottled paint surfaces made with destructive methods, such as scraping them with meat cleavers; whereas Westermann created sculptures in the 1950s that are small scaled, neat and precise, hand tooled, and sometimes gamelike or participatory (see fig. 2), and his works on paper featured jocular, antihero avatars based on contemporary and tragicomic characters, such as Dick Tracy, Popeye, and a Rhett Butler–type Casanova.[7] Although Westermann exuded strength and confidence in life—he maintained an impressive physique following his military service, worked as a part-time artist's model at SAIC, and was known to display

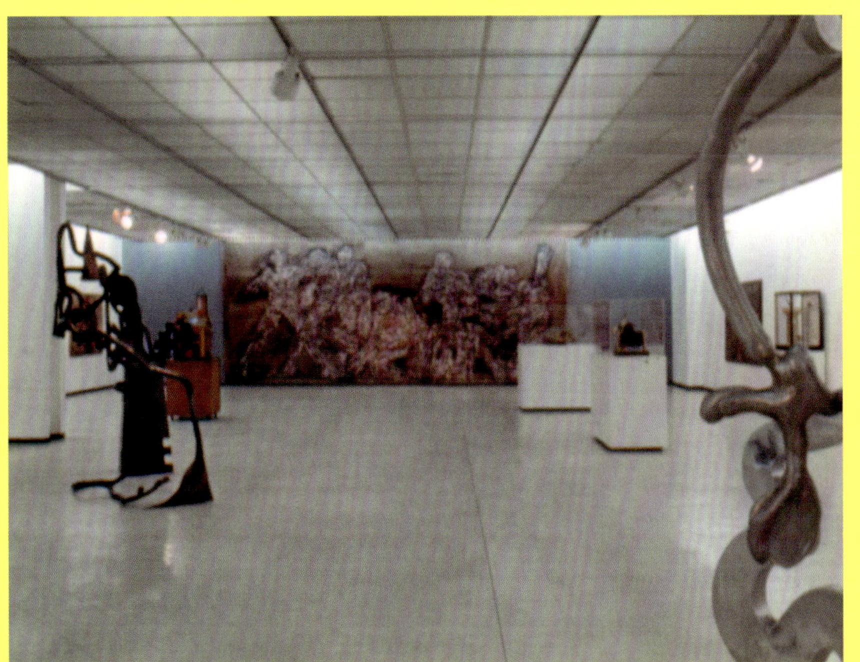

FIG. 2
INSTALLATION VIEW OF *CHICAGO IMAGIST ART*, MUSEUM OF CONTEMPORARY ART CHICAGO, MAY 13–JUNE 25, 1972.

Golub's painting *Gigantomachy I* (1965; Museum of Modern Art, New York) on the far wall dwarfs Westermann's sculpture *Mad House* (1957; Museum of Contemporary Art Chicago) in the back left.

his athleticism as a party trick—his early sculptural works, such as *He-Whore* (1957; Museum of Contemporary Art Chicago) and *Male, American* (1957; Alan and Dorothy Press Collection, Chicago), convey vulnerability and self-doubt while also reflecting his anxiety about, or skepticism of, traditional masculine ideals.[8] Golub's epic imagery may have helped define the Monster Roster, but Westermann's humorous yet critical take on the prevailing postwar optimism about America's abundance and virility resonated with younger artists.

The various aspects of Westermann's work that distanced it from the Monster Roster—his unvarnished autobiographical or narrative content, his unabashed admiration for and integration of vernacular culture, and his graphic lexicon, which incorporated cartoons and comics—were the same qualities that appealed to the artists dubbed the Chicago Imagists in 1972, including Sarah Canright, Ed Flood, Art Green, Gladys Nilsson, and Jim Nutt, among others. SAIC alumna Cynthia Carlson succinctly conveyed Westermann's impact on these artists, stating, "He gave us the courage to be ourselves."[9] Encouraged by his example, they continued to develop their own varied practices in spite of their shared educational backgrounds, exhibition histories, and gallery representation. Art historian Whitney Halstead concretized this relationship in his 1974 catalogue essay for the Museum of Contemporary Art Chicago's Imagist show: "The work of one artist, H. C. Westermann, forecasts the direction and provides a keynote [for the Imagists]. In part as influence, always as model, his achievement was of enormous importance for these artists, for it demonstrated that an artist following his own bent could evolve an art of great expressive power apart from the main tradition, separate from the mainstream."[10]

Westermann's work was so far from the mainstream that Nutt recalled his shock upon first encountering one of his sculptures, which exploded his ideas about labels and categories:

> One afternoon I went to the Frumkin Gallery.…I wandered into
> a back room and was startled to be face to face with an imposing
> wooden object, which had an immaculate steam pressure
> gauge at the very top. "Yikes?!" was my first thought followed
> with, "This isn't Fine Art!"…Had I been aware of its title, *Object
> Under Pressure* [pl. 2], I probably would have been even more
> confused than I already was.…Struggle as I might, I didn't
> come close to squeezing it into any of the art history pigeonholes
> I was familiar with.[11]

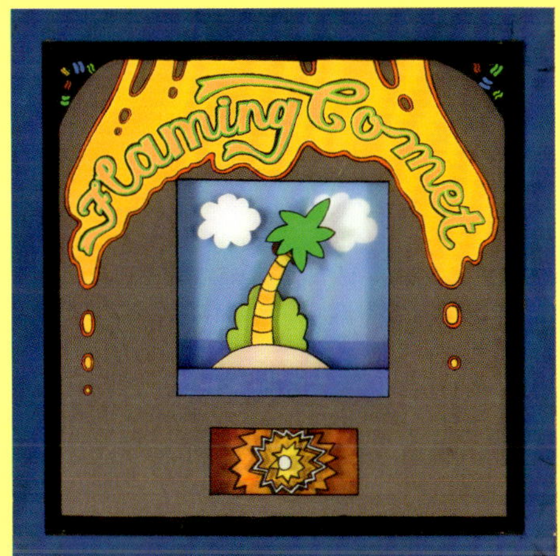

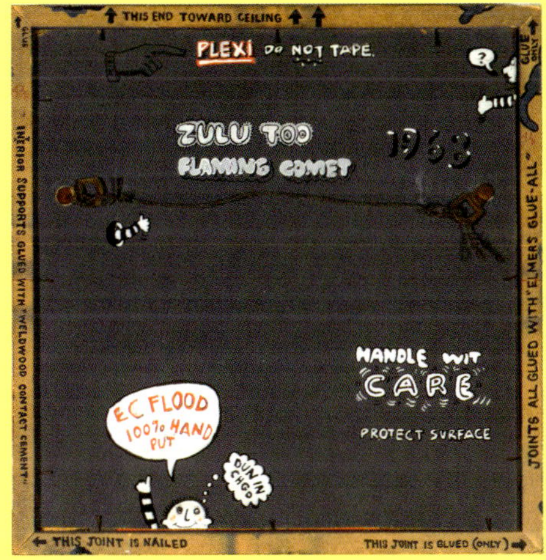

Nutt's eventual employment as an art preparator at Frumkin's gallery gave him the opportunity to handle Westermann's work and closely observe its beguiling intricacies: glyphs, haptic elements, hatches, peepholes, small inscriptions, and, in later works, hand-carved or stamped annotations about the media employed in a piece (see p. 53) and hefty custom crates that could double as display furniture. The impact of this experience is evident in Nutt's early paintings, which likewise feature collaged ephemera and stamped metal hardware, as in *Miss E. Knows* (1967; Art Institute of Chicago), and shaped support surfaces or frames, as in *Wowidow* (1968; Art Institute of Chicago).

Westermann created his sculpture using materials and methods informed by his experiences as a handyman, a side job that kept him afloat while he pursued his art degree. Examples of the hardware and home-repair materials in his sculptures include Astroturf, caster wheels, chain, faucets, galvanized sheet metal, hydrostone, pipes and valves, reflectors, security wire glass, and weather vents.[12] And his skillful construction demonstrates techniques "usually associated more with tradesmen than with contemporary artists—including wood joinery, upholstery, and metalsmithing," as well as dovetailing, hand-carving, and lamination.[13] The artist's "blue-collar" materials and techniques share similarities with the work of Ed Flood, a friend and fellow artist who also gigged as a handyman, and the two were known to exchange tools as well as intricately illustrated letters. Some have argued that Westermann's early box-like constructions, like *The Night Life* (pl. 5), inspired Flood's layered Plexiglas paintings slotted into wooden shadow-box frames, such as *Zulu Too Flaming Comet* (fig. 3), whose verso is covered with instructions on how to handle and display the piece in a manner reminiscent of a Westermann.[14]

Westermann also influenced Chicago artists with his politics, especially a young Green, who lived in the city while studying at SAIC. Although they never met, Green looked

8. SAIC alumnus Irving Petlin recalled, "He would take his shirt off and stand on his hands, and he could make the bluebirds (tattooed on his pectoral muscles) kiss each other." Irving Petlin, interview transcript from Leslie Buchbinder, dir., *Westermann: Memorial to the Idea of Man If He Was an Idea* (Chicago: Pentimenti Productions, 2023), courtesy of Pentimenti Productions.

9. Cynthia Carlson, phone call with the author, Dec. 13, 2023.

10. Whitney Halstead, "Made in Chicago," in *Made in Chicago*, exh. cat. (Washington, DC: National Collection of Fine Arts by the Smithsonian Institution Press, 1974), 12.

11. Jim Nutt, quoted in Michael Rooks, *Dreaming of a Speech Without Words: The Paintings and Early Objects of H. C. Westermann* (Honolulu: The Contemporary Museum, 2006), 101.

12. Westermann also used linoleum in several sculptures in the 1960s, including *The Hands* (1961; Nelson-Atkins Museum of Art, Kansas City, MO), *Machine for Calculating Risks* (1962; Billy Al Bengston, Los Angeles), and *Wet Flower* (pl. 11).

13. Chicago Art Before The Hairy Who, IV. Influential Early Artists, chicagoimagists .com/#milestones/chicagoartbefore thehairywho, accessed Mar. 2, 2024.

14. For more on the relationship between Ed Flood and Westermann, see Robert Storr, "Tropical Isles for a Cold Climate," in *Ed Flood: Constructions; Boxes and Works on Paper, 1967–1973* (Chicago: Corbett vs. Dempsey, 2009), 7.

back on this impact decades later: "I was deeply impressed by his work and his independence in clearing his own path. I remember looking long and often at his *Mysteriously Abandoned New Home* at the AIC—and I often saw his work at Frumkin's [gallery]....His work, drawn from episodes in his life which were rooted in larger global geo-political conflicts into which he was thrust…encouraged me to include [in my work] Secretary McNamara, one of the authors of the Vietnam adventure, which threatened to involve me (also against my will) at the time."[15] An outlier in Green's body of work, *Examine the Facts, Consider the Options, Apply the Logic* (fig. 4) illustrates the way Westermann broke through to a younger generation of Chicago artists, as both a model they looked up to and a counterpart with overlapping experiences and sentiments.

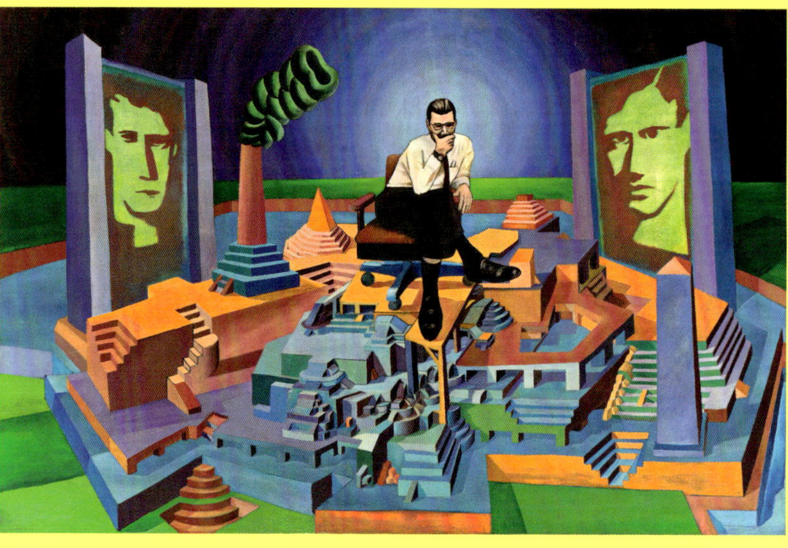

FIG. 4
ART GREEN (AMERICAN, BORN 1941). *EXAMINE THE FACTS, CONSIDER THE OPTIONS, APPLY THE LOGIC*, 1965–66. OIL AND ACRYLIC ON CANVAS; 172.1 × 266.2 CM (67¾ × 104¹³⁄₁₆ IN.). MUSEUM OF CONTEMPORARY ART CHICAGO, GIFT OF DENNIS ADRIAN AND PHYLLIS KIND IN HONOR OF THE ARTIST.

Green based the title on a quote by the Vietnam War–era US Secretary of Defense Robert McNamara.

Running parallel with artistic developments in Chicago, Westermann made inroads through Dilexi Gallery in Los Angeles and San Francisco—where artists such as William T. Wiley first encountered his work—and these were reenforced by his return to his native California a handful of times. In 1964 Westermann and Beall drove cross-country in the "batmobile" (his name for a souped-up pickup truck embellished with a hood ornament he cast himself) to San Francisco, where the pair lived for a year before moving back permanently to Connecticut. The next year, Wiley and Bruce Nauman began corresponding with Westermann by mail.[16] He later relocated temporarily to Los Angeles for an eight-week artist residency at the Tamarind Lithography Workshop in 1968, which put him in direct contact with Billy Al Bengston, Ken Price (see p. 28), and Ed Ruscha, and to San Francisco for a short-term teaching position at the San Francisco Art Institute in 1970. The impression Westermann made on

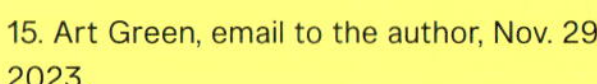

15. Art Green, email to the author, Nov. 29, 2023.

16. For more on the initial exchange between Westermann and Nauman and Wiley, see page 16 of this volume.

17. Ed Ruscha, interview transcript from Buchbinder, *Westermann: Memorial to the Idea*, courtesy of Pentimenti Productions. For more on Nauman's works related to Westermann, see pages 16–17 of this volume.

18. Ruscha, interview transcript from Buchbinder, *Westermann: Memorial to the Idea*, courtesy of Pentimenti Productions. For more on Ruscha's initial impressions of Westermann, see page 21 of this volume.

19. Westermann and Beall helped Ken and Happy Price relocate to Taos, New Mexico, in 1970. Happy Price, interview transcript from Buchbinder, *Westermann: Memorial to the Idea*, courtesy of Pentimenti Productions.

these artists comes through in the many works he directly inspired, as in the titular wordplay and visual pun of Robert Arneson's sculpture *Head Stand on a Cliff* (1985; Estate of Robert Arneson); the caricatured cameo of Westermann himself in *Bloated Empire, Stuffed Regime* (fig. 5), which Ruscha based on a desire to "somehow grasp some of his thinking, and inject it into my work…almost like a collaboration of sorts"; and the honorific memorials to Westermann as an artist and to his artwork in Nauman's sculpture *Westermann's Ear* (see p. 16, fig. 5) and drawing *Square Knot (H. C. Westermann)* (1967; collection of the artist).[17]

Ruscha, who met Westermann at social events during his residency at Tamarind, recalled the way the artist's theatrical physicality captured the attention of his peers: "He had an inclination to show off to people in his quiet way…he would do handstands, and walk across the room, made sure he had plenty of spare change in his pockets so it spilled all over the floor and ran everywhere, and he'd be smoking a long cigar while he was at it…it [was] a perfect little piece of performance art."[18] His acrobatic stunts (see p. 20) recall developments in the burgeoning field of performance art, sharing something in common with Nauman's early performances, such as *Walking in an Exaggerated Manner around the Perimeter of a Square* (1967–68), which were similarly task oriented, if more mundane.

Westermann's politics also resonated with many of these artists: the anti-war stance he developed during the Korean War was echoed by the younger generation's opposition to the Vietnam War. His slow, handmade approach to art making appealed to the custom car and surf cultural vernacular in Southern California that gave birth to Finish Fetish, a term that encompasses the meticulous creations of Bengston. And his proto-environmentalism resonated with the back-to-the-land leanings of several other artists—such as Ken Price, whom Westermann, together with Happy Price, convinced to move to the country in order "to not be a part of an art scene" but instead be "devoted to working, and also to sky, and clean air, and nature."[19]

The time Westermann spent in California led to friendships with artists who shared not only his politics but also many of his artistic impulses: His linguistic play, which manifested in malapropisms,

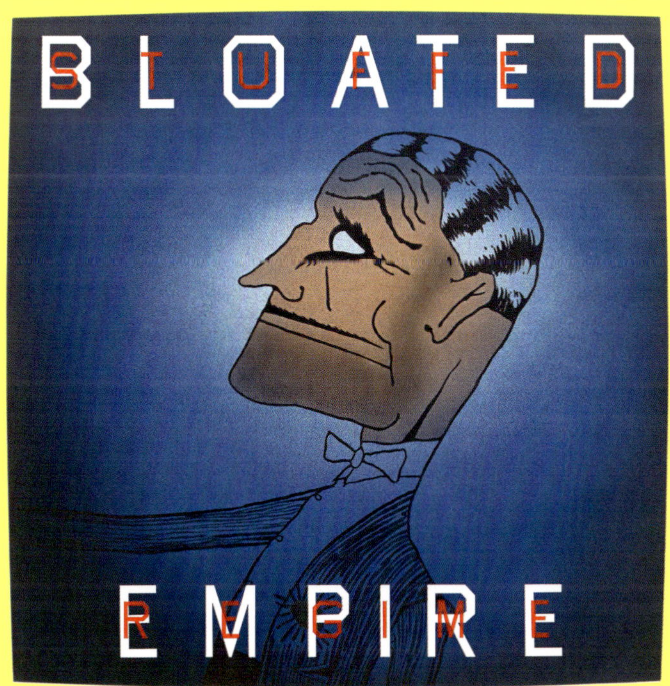

FIG. 5
ED RUSCHA (AMERICAN, BORN 1937). *BLOATED EMPIRE, STUFFED REGIME*, 1997. ACRYLIC ON SHAPED CANVAS: 193 × 196.9 CM (76 × 77½ IN.). COURTESY OF VENUS OVER MANHATTAN.

Ruscha copied the portrait in profile from Westermann's illustration of his dandy persona (see fig. 7 of this essay).

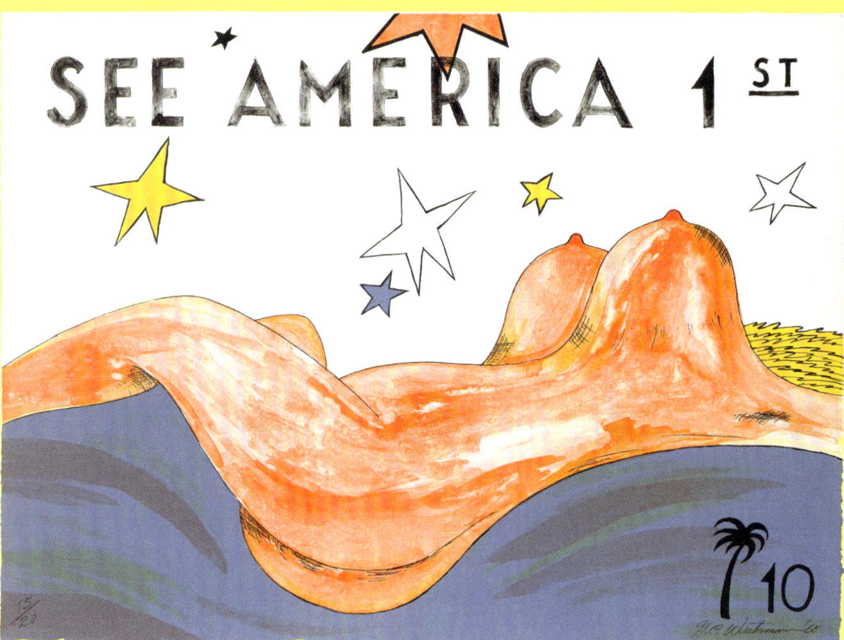

FIG. 6
WESTERMANN, PRINTED BY MAURICE
SÁNCHEZ (AMERICAN, BORN 1945),
PUBLISHED BY TAMARIND LITHOGRAPHY
WORKSHOP (AMERICAN, 1960–1976).
UNTITLED, PLATE TEN FROM *SEE
AMERICA FIRST*, 1968. COLOR
LITHOGRAPH ON PAPER: 55.9 × 76.5 CM
(22⅟₁₆ × 30⅛ IN.). THE ART INSTITUTE
OF CHICAGO, PURCHASED WITH FUNDS
PROVIDED BY DOROTHY AND ALAN
PRESS, 1992.10.10.

wordplay, and coded inscriptions or titles (such as *Le Kequee [After Jockomedy]* [1966; Ann Janis, Los Angeles]) reflected Ruscha's initial focus on the relationship between art and language in the production of "visual non-sequiturs."[20] His self-deprecating and slapstick self-portraiture finds apt comparisons in the ribald works Arneson created using his own body and likeness and in the raunchy humor and irreverence of Peter Saul's politically charged paintings from this same moment. And his material choices, which often reflected his anti-consumerist ethos, resonated with the novel materials and concepts of Price's functional ceramics—a craft he recontextualized as fine art—and Wiley's provisional assemblages created from studio tools and debris (both fitting comparisons with the thrifted "Slant Step," a decades-long in-joke perpetuated by Arneson, Nauman, and Wiley that celebrated the ambiguity and obsolescence of a humorous found object).

Westermann's own sense of humor—which could be dark and was often more forlorn than funny—is vividly pronounced in his drawings and prints, which have been compared to the narrative yet hallucinatory work of Bay Area–based artist Roy De Forest. Westermann's works on paper comprise prints he created over a fifteen-year period and drawings tucked away in sketchbooks and personal correspondence, and this lesser-known or private facet of his practice led him to Tamarind.[21] During his residency,

Westermann—lonely and longing for his wife—commemorated their earlier trip to San Francisco in *See America First* (see fig. 6), a portfolio of seventeen lithographs and one frontispiece. Cheekily titled after, and emblazoned with, the national tourism slogan, the prints depict a warped version of its propagandistic meaning, reflecting Westermann's perspective as a grizzled, world-weary veteran who saw through the mythical idealization of national identity.

FROM HIS HOME IN CONNECTICUT, WESTERMANN RELIED ON THE US Postal Service for communicating with artists. His dedication to the slow, personalized, and semi-private practice of sending mail is evinced by the numerous illustrated letters he exchanged with artists in California and in Chicago, including Flood and Canright (see fig. 7). He was even known to respond to strangers, often young artists eager to connect with him. Among them was Ray Johnson, the pioneer of the concurrently developing mail art movement, who provides an illuminating contrast. Johnson became known for maintaining mysterious, acerbic, and sometimes competitive exchanges with numerous correspondents who either reciprocated or found themselves excluded from future mailings; Westermann's letters by contrast were generous and sincere, almost to the point of vulnerability, combining the goofy, gory, and caricatured iconography of his print work with calligraphic missives and confessions, forming what art historian Max Kozloff described as "a genuine comic-strip of his psyche."[22]

This intimate form of communication became especially important to Westermann later in his career, as he grew increasingly frustrated by and skeptical of the art world. His mailings of letters but also handcrafted gifts (see p. 24, fig. 3)—allowed him to carry on private exchanges directly with the artists he admired, further blurring the boundaries between art and life, subverting definitions of what constituted an art object, and circumnavigating the critical or public sphere, as well as the commercial gallery system. The intricate and unexpected presents Westermann mailed out gained him a reputation for producing "two hundred gifts every year, and about three works of art"—although

20. I borrowed this term from Russell Bowman, who used it to describe the work of René Magritte in the context of art and language. Russell Bowman, "Words and Images: A Persistent Paradox," *Art Journal* 45, no. 4 (Winter 1985): 336.

21. For more on Westermann's printmaking practice, including at Chicago's Landfall Press, see Dennis Adrian and Richard A. Born, *See America First: The Prints of H. C. Westermann* (Chicago: David and Alfred Smart Museum of Art, University of Chicago, 2001).

22. Max Kozloff, "Junk Mail: An Affluent Art Movement," *Art Journal* 33, no. 1 (Autumn 1973): 28.

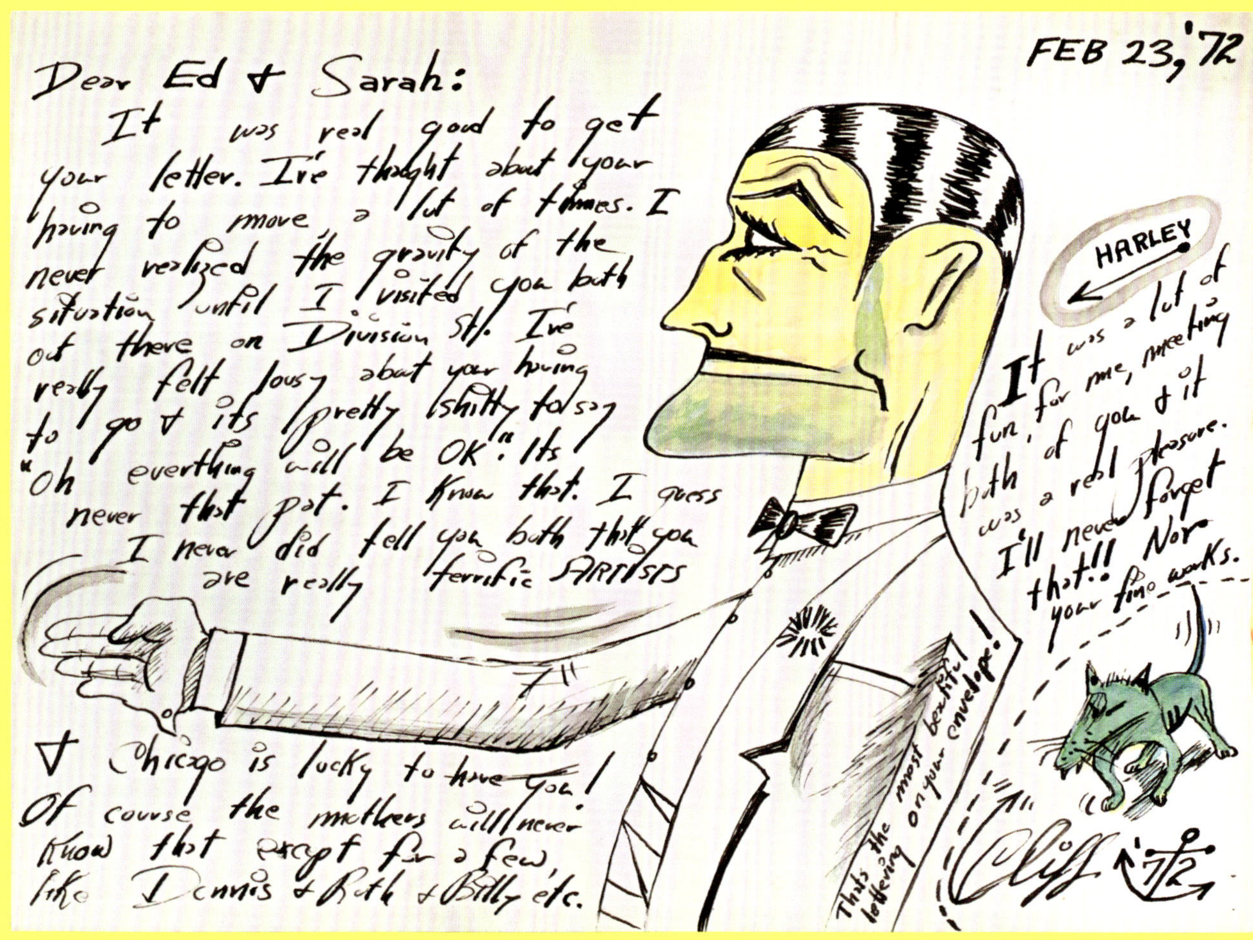
FEB 23, '72
Dear Ed & Sarah:
It was real good to get your letter. I've thought about your having to move a lot of times. I never realized the gravity of the situation until I visited you both out there on Division St. I've really felt lousy about your having to go & its pretty shitty to say "Oh everything will be OK". Its never that pat. I know that. I guess I never did tell you both that you are really terrific ARTISTS
& Chicago is lucky to have you! Of course the mothers will never know that except for a few, like Dennis & Ruth & Billy etc.
HARLEY
It was a lot of fun for me, meeting both of you & it was a real pleasure. I'll never forget that!! Now your fine works.
This is the most beautiful lettering on your envelop.

it is difficult to distinguish the gifted objects from artworks, even with his insistence on their use value, whether the contents comprised a dustpan that he created in 1966 for critic Dennis Adrian or three cans of varnish he encased in a handcrafted box for Ruscha in 1976.[23] Just as many of his works function as memorials—such as *Memorial to the Idea of Man If He Was an Idea* (1958; Museum of Contemporary Art Chicago) and his numerous "mausoleums"—these pieces often honor or commemorate specific people, as in *Nothing Is to Be Done for William T. Wiley* (1967; William T. Wiley, Woodacre, CA); *Le Bandeur* (1969; Sharon and Thurston Twigg-Smith, Honolulu), a gift to Serge Lozingot, a printer he met at the Tamarind residency; and *Untitled (for Happy Price)* (c. 1975; location unknown). As a result, these objects register the relationships he valued most.[24]

Westermann championed an unconventional index of sources and represented an alternative professionalism that captured the imaginations of a younger generation of artists in Chicago and California, encouraging them to reject labels imposed on them, draw on personal experiences to address broader cultural attitudes, and carve their own paths through the art world. Interpreted initially as "separate from the mainstream," his art ultimately ran parallel to major developments in postwar American art, just as his relationships linked him to a broad swath of postwar American artists. Although he did not fit the art historical mold, Westermann—with his unapologetic independence that fueled a singular body of work—provided a powerful model for an equally diverse and radical generation. ⚓

23. Ruscha, interview from Buchbinder, *Westermann: Memorial to the Idea*, courtesy of Pentimenti Productions.

24. For more on these specific objects, see Michael Rooks and Lynne Warren, eds., *H. C. Westermann: Exhibition Catalogue and Catalogue Raisonné of Objects* (Chicago: Museum of Contemporary Art Chicago in association with Harry N. Abrams, 2001).

PLATES

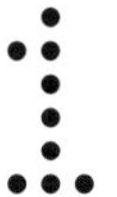

UNCOMMITTED
LITTLE
CHICAGO CHILD

1957
OAK, MAPLE, METAL CLOCKFACE,
AND PAPER DECOUPAGE

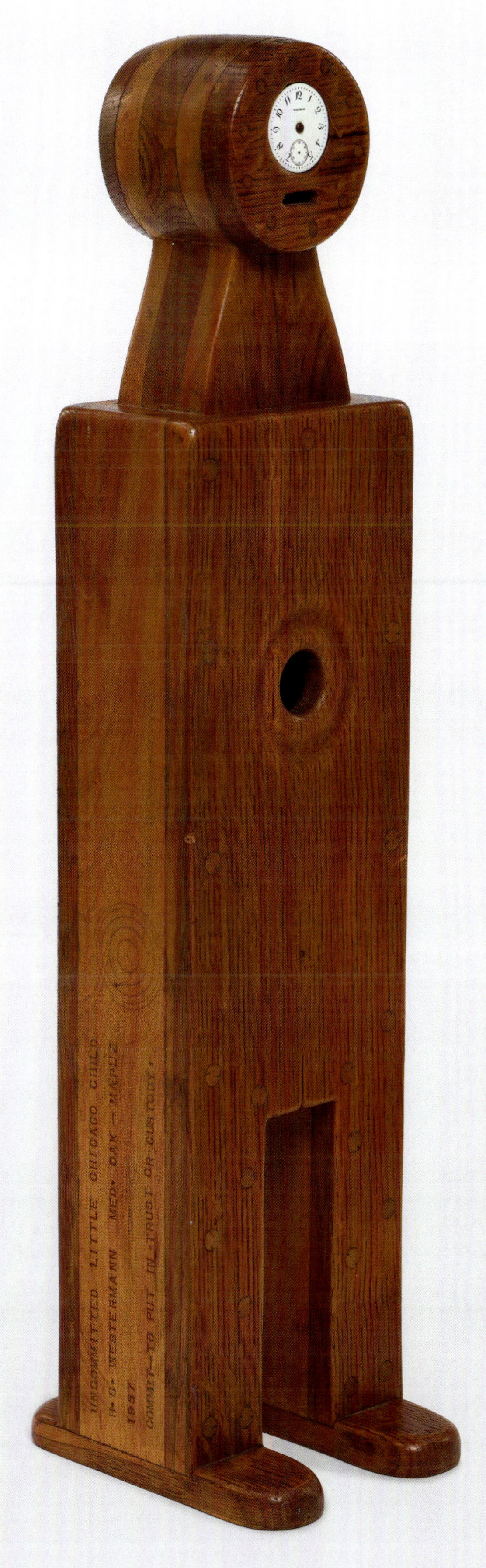
UNCOMMITTED "LITTLE CHICAGO CHILD"
H. C. WESTERMANN   MED. OAK — MAPLE
1937
COMMIT — TO PUT IN TRUST OR CUSTODY.

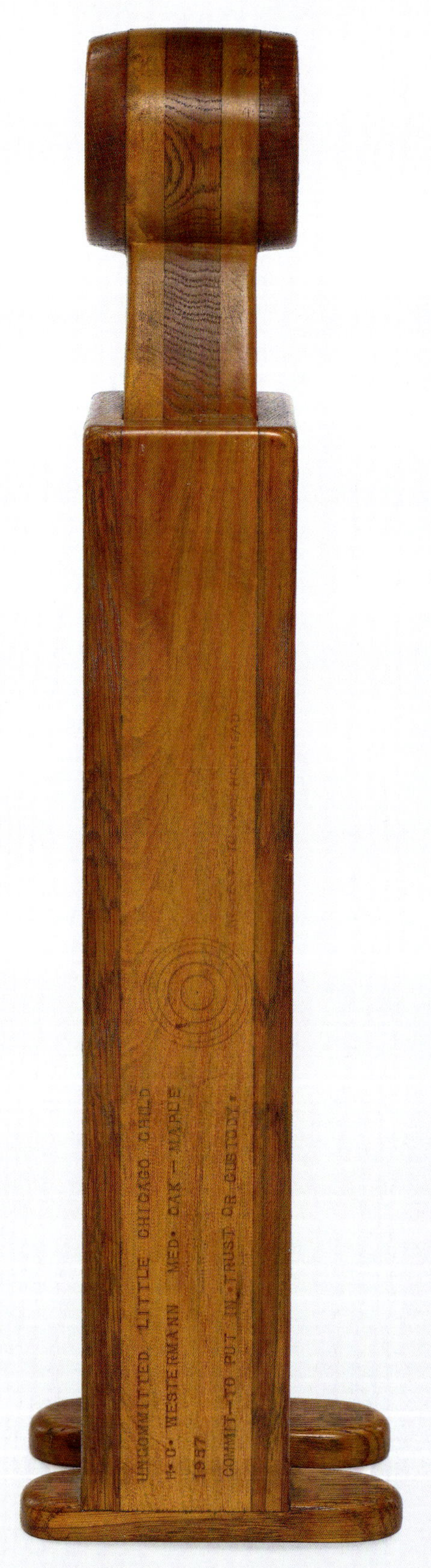

UNCOMMITTED LITTLE CHICAGO CHILD
H. C. WESTERMANN MED. OAK — MAPLE
1957
COMMIT—TO PUT IN TRUST OR CUSTODY.

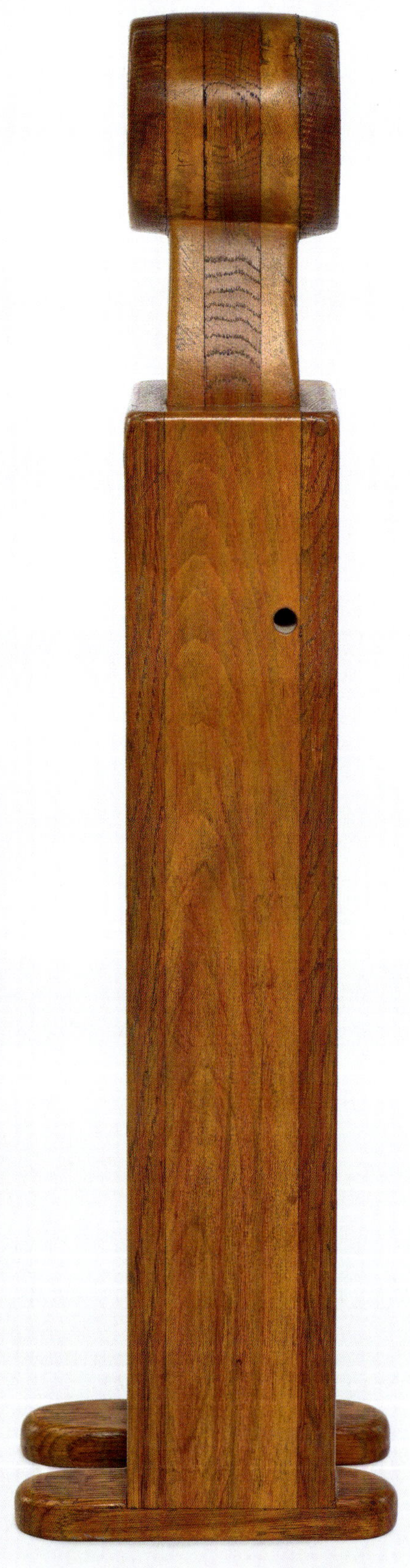

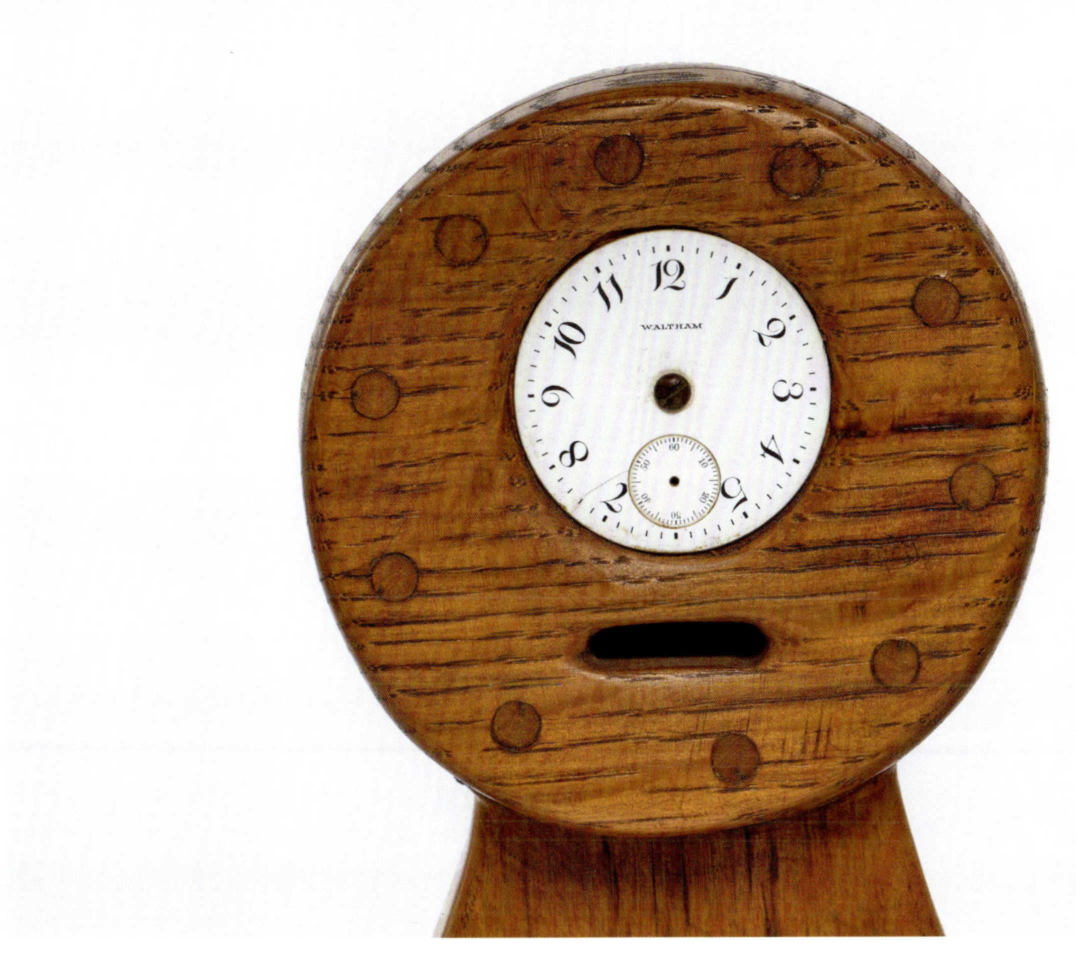

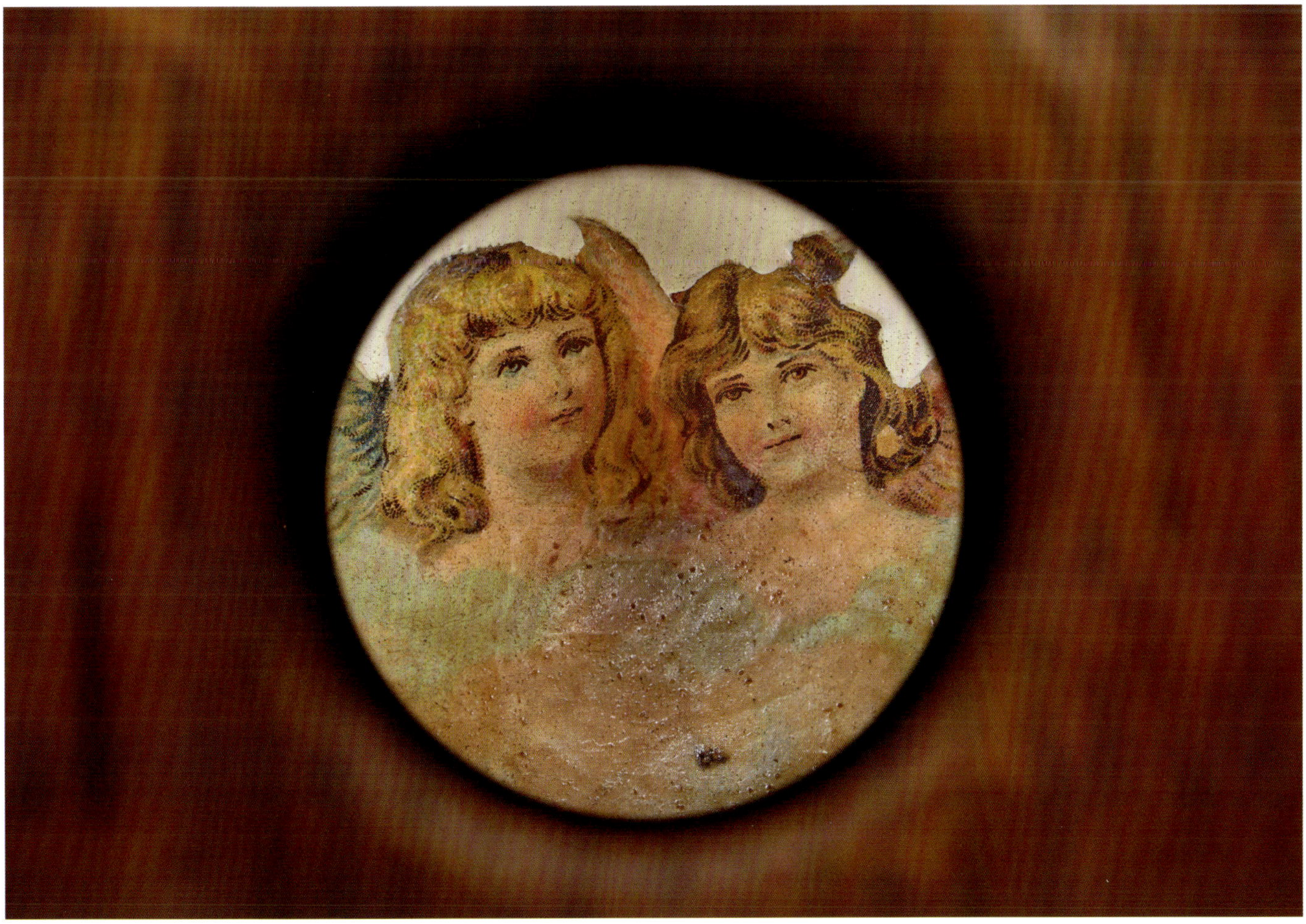

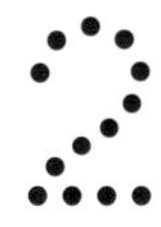

OBJECT UNDER
PRESSURE

1960
DOUGLAS FIR, METAL,
AND PRESSURE GAUGE

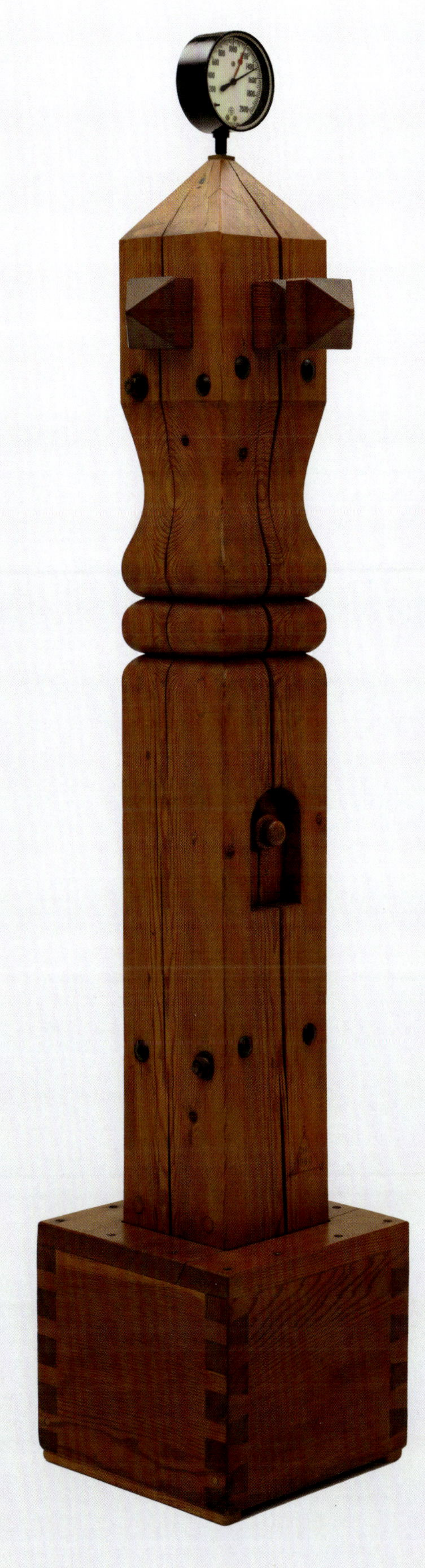

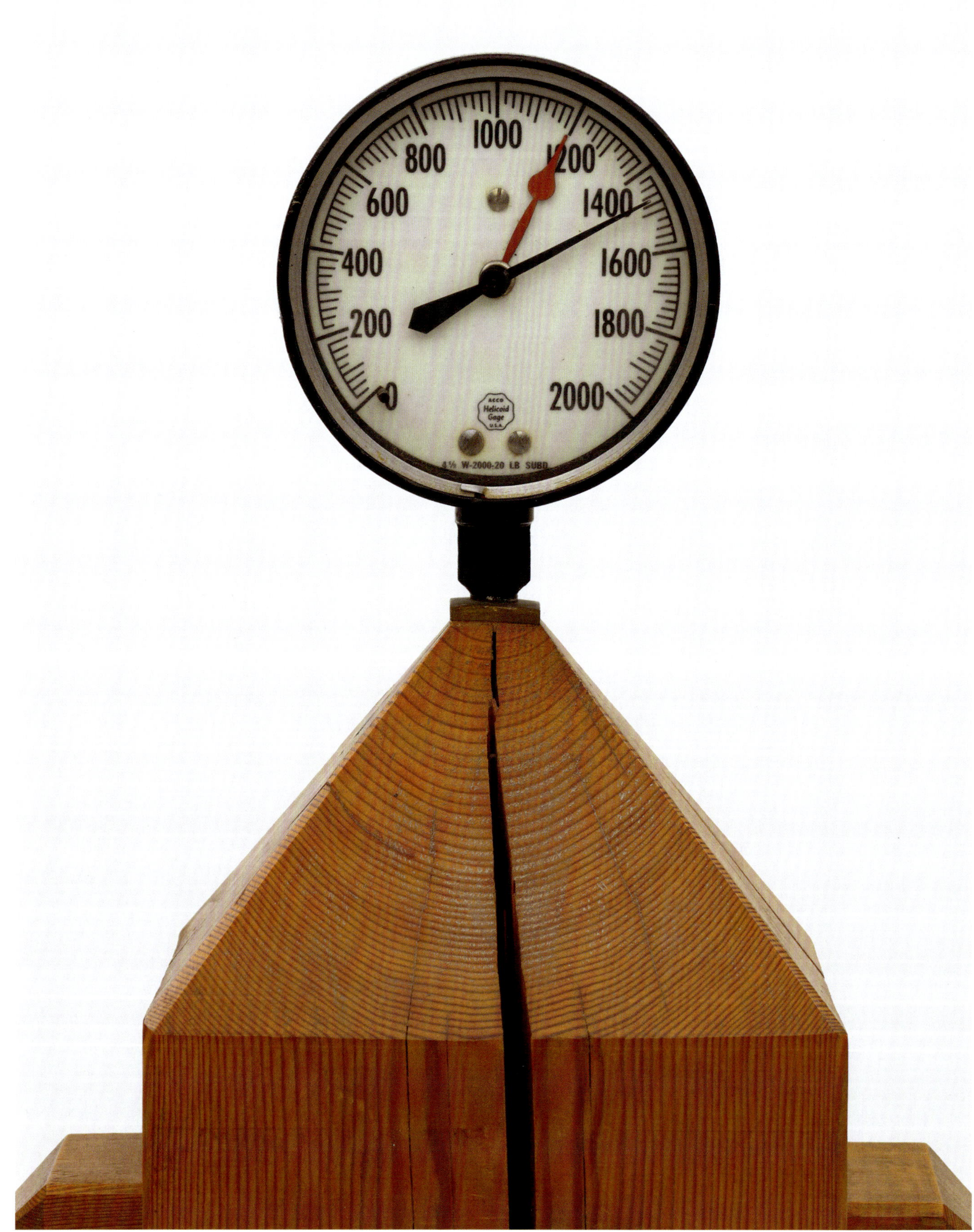
800 1000 1200
600 1400
400 1600
200 1800
0 2000
ACCO
Helicoid
Gage
U.S.A.
4 ½ W-2000-20 LB SUBD

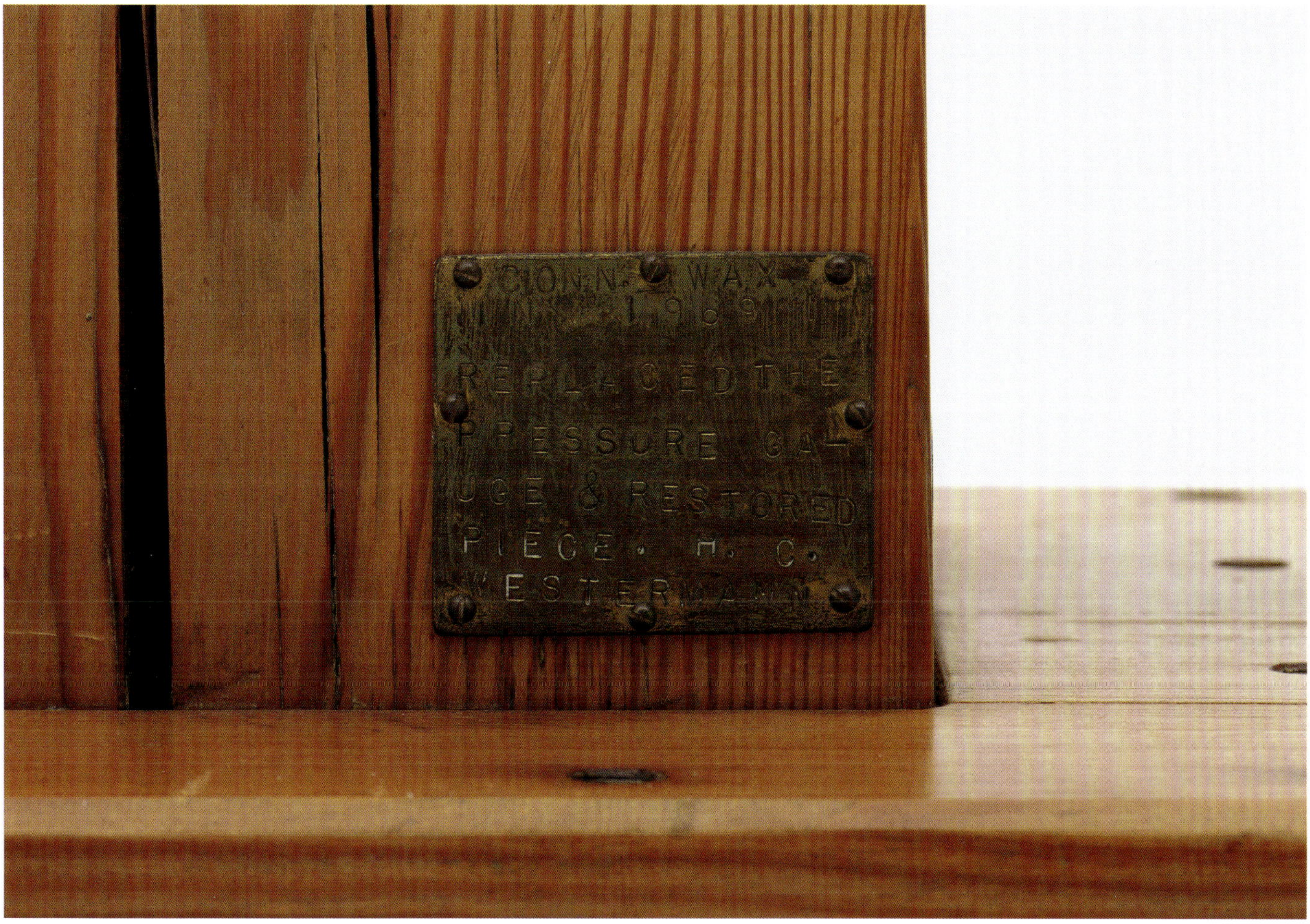

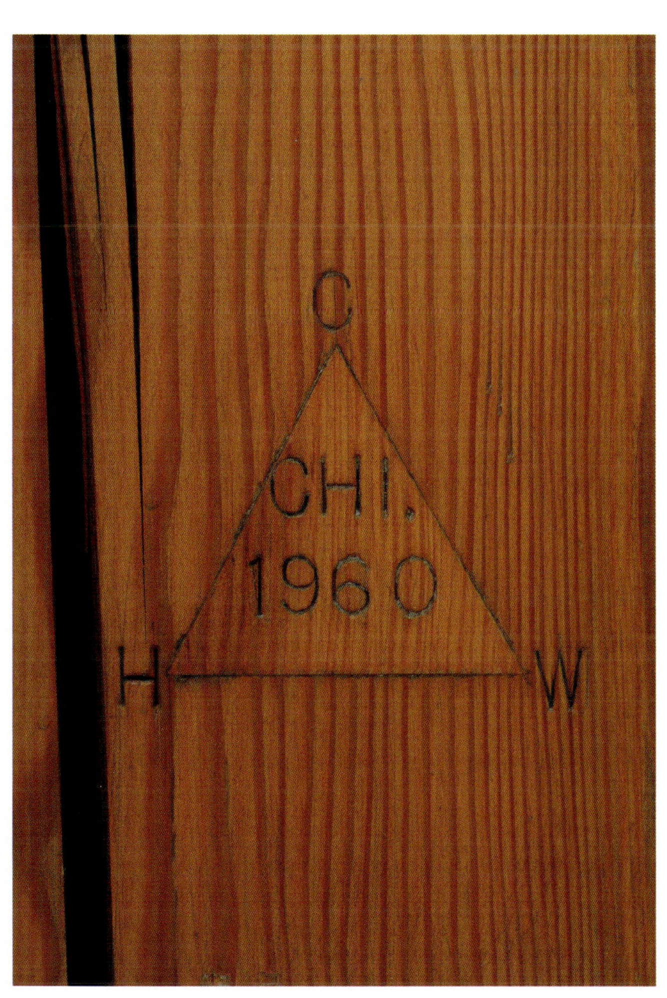
CONN. WAX
IN. 1969
REPLACED THE
PRESSURE GAU
GE & RESTORED
PIECE. M. C.
WESTERMAN

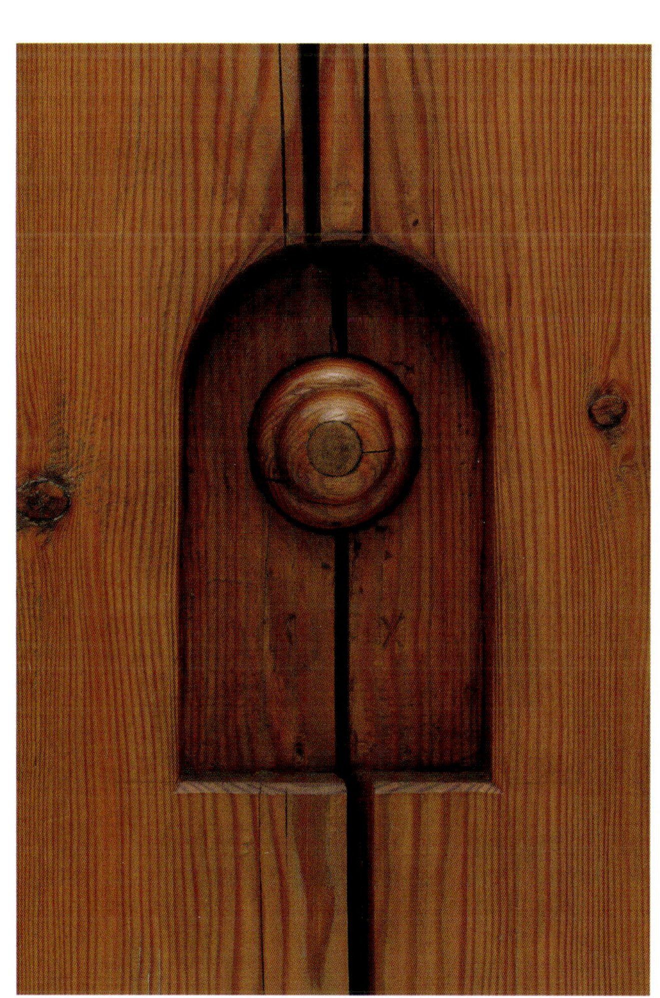
C
CHI.
1960
H   W

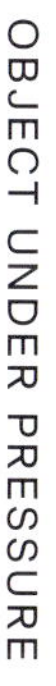

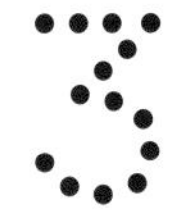

THE BIG CHANGE

1963
DOUGLAS FIR MARINE PLYWOOD,
MASONITE, AND INK

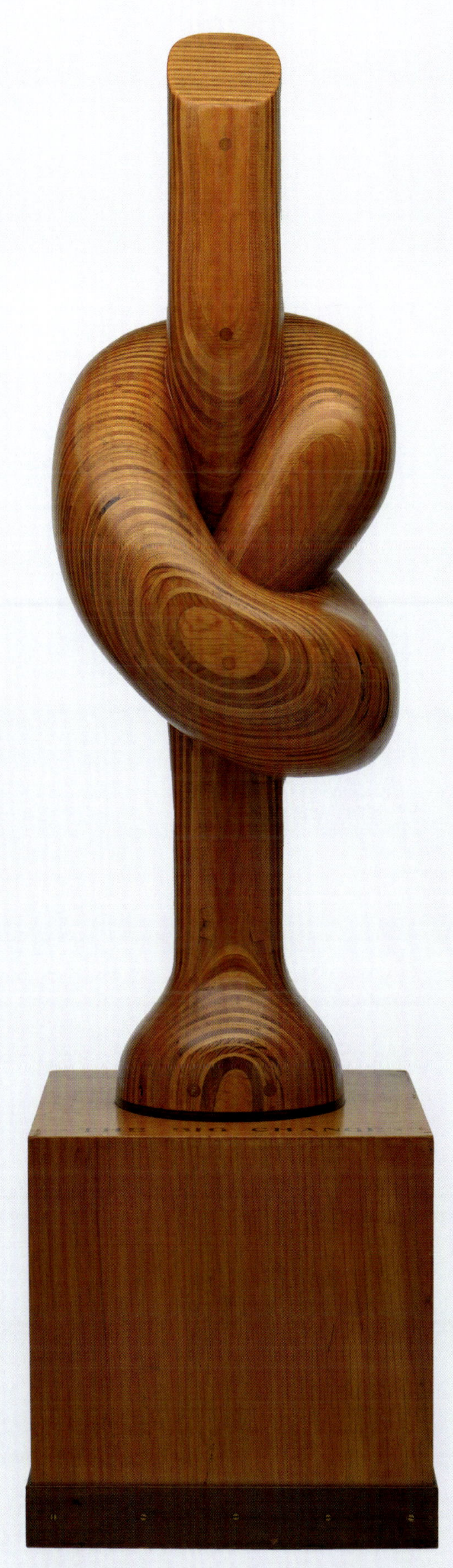
THE BIG CHANGE

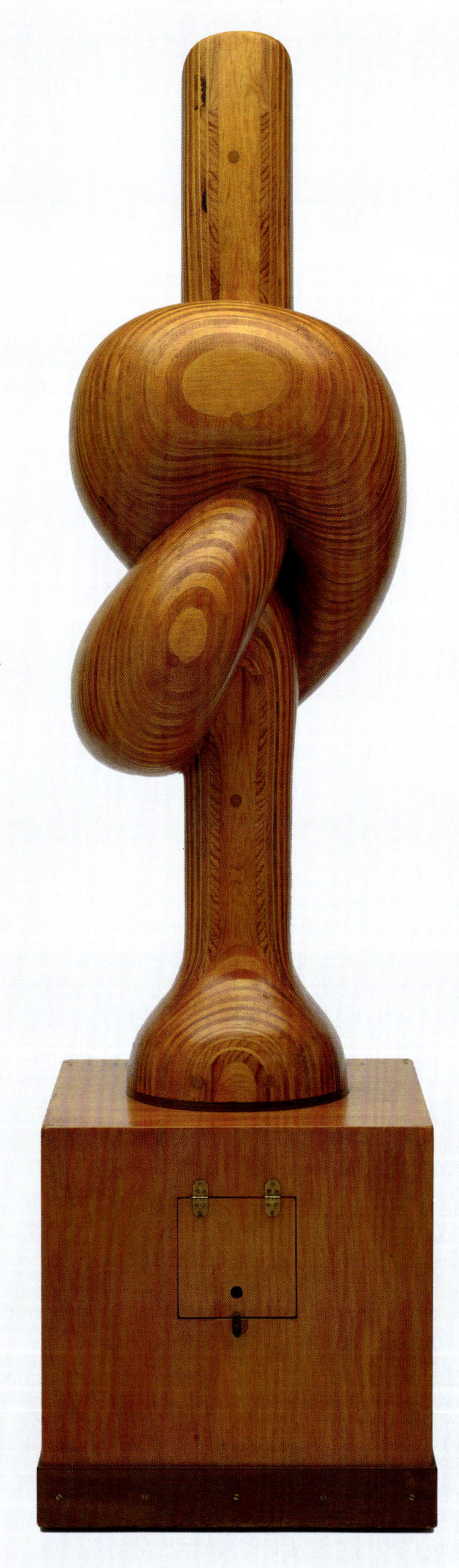

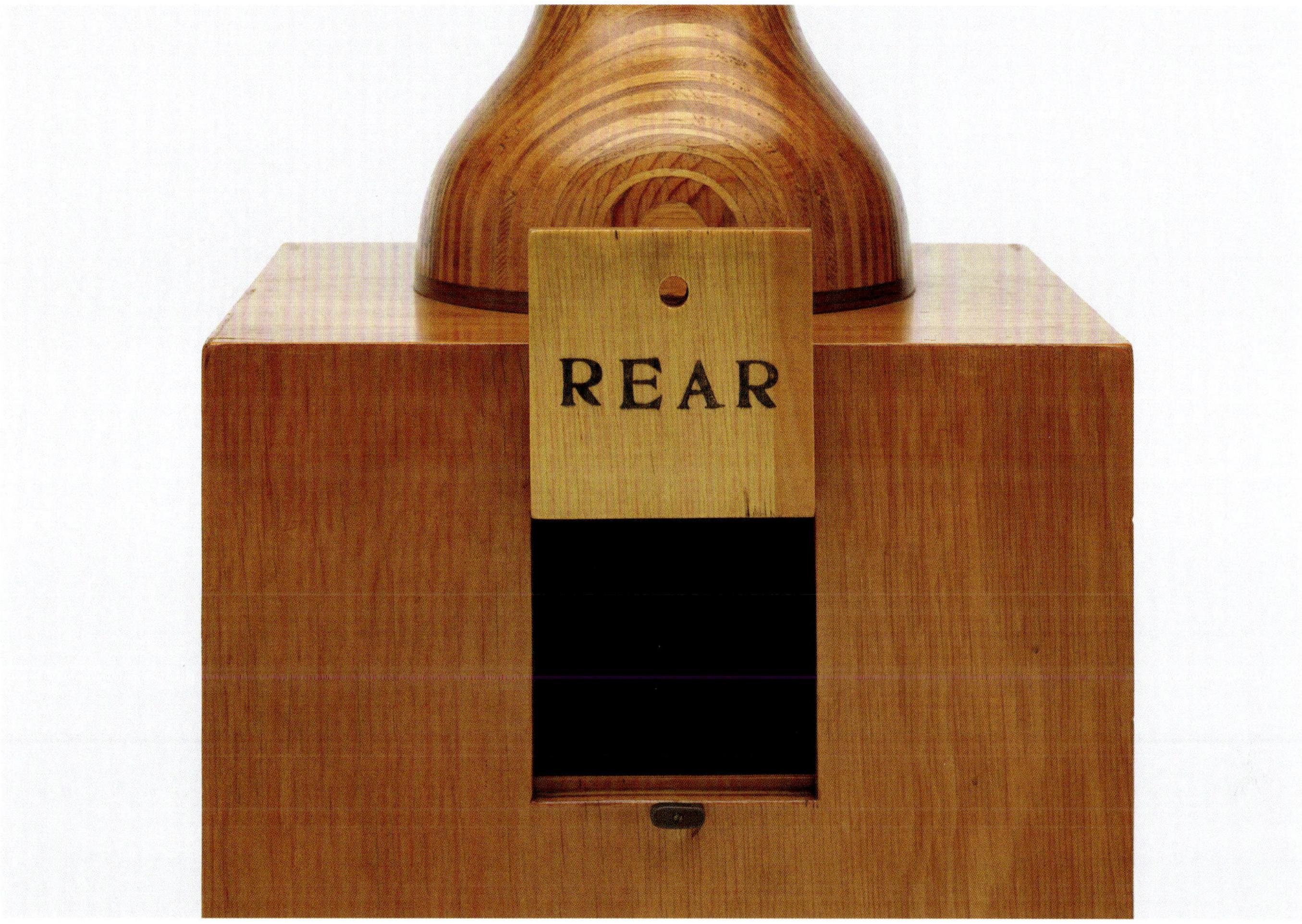

REAR

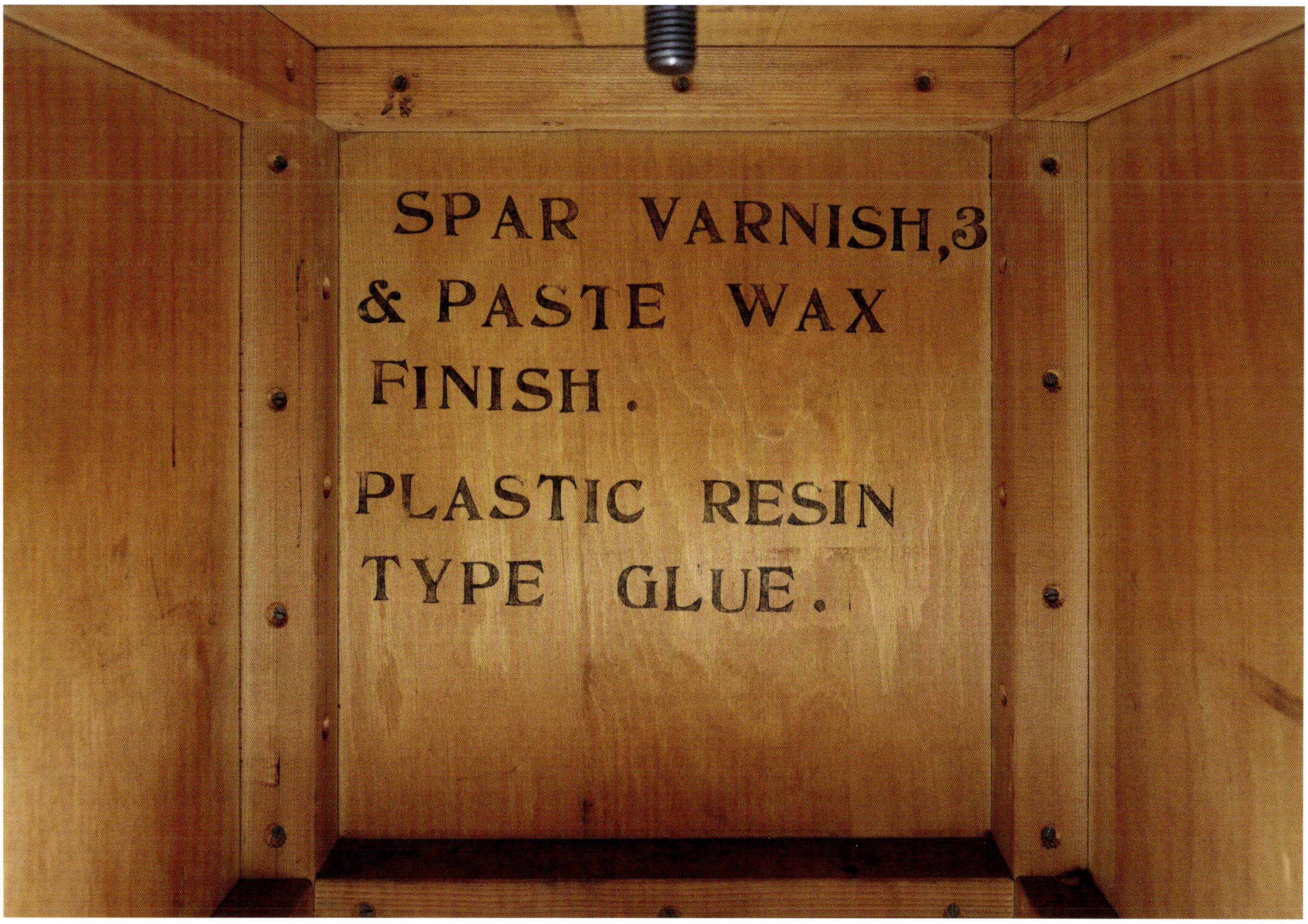

SPAR VARNISH,3
& PASTE WAX
FINISH.

PLASTIC RESIN
TYPE GLUE.

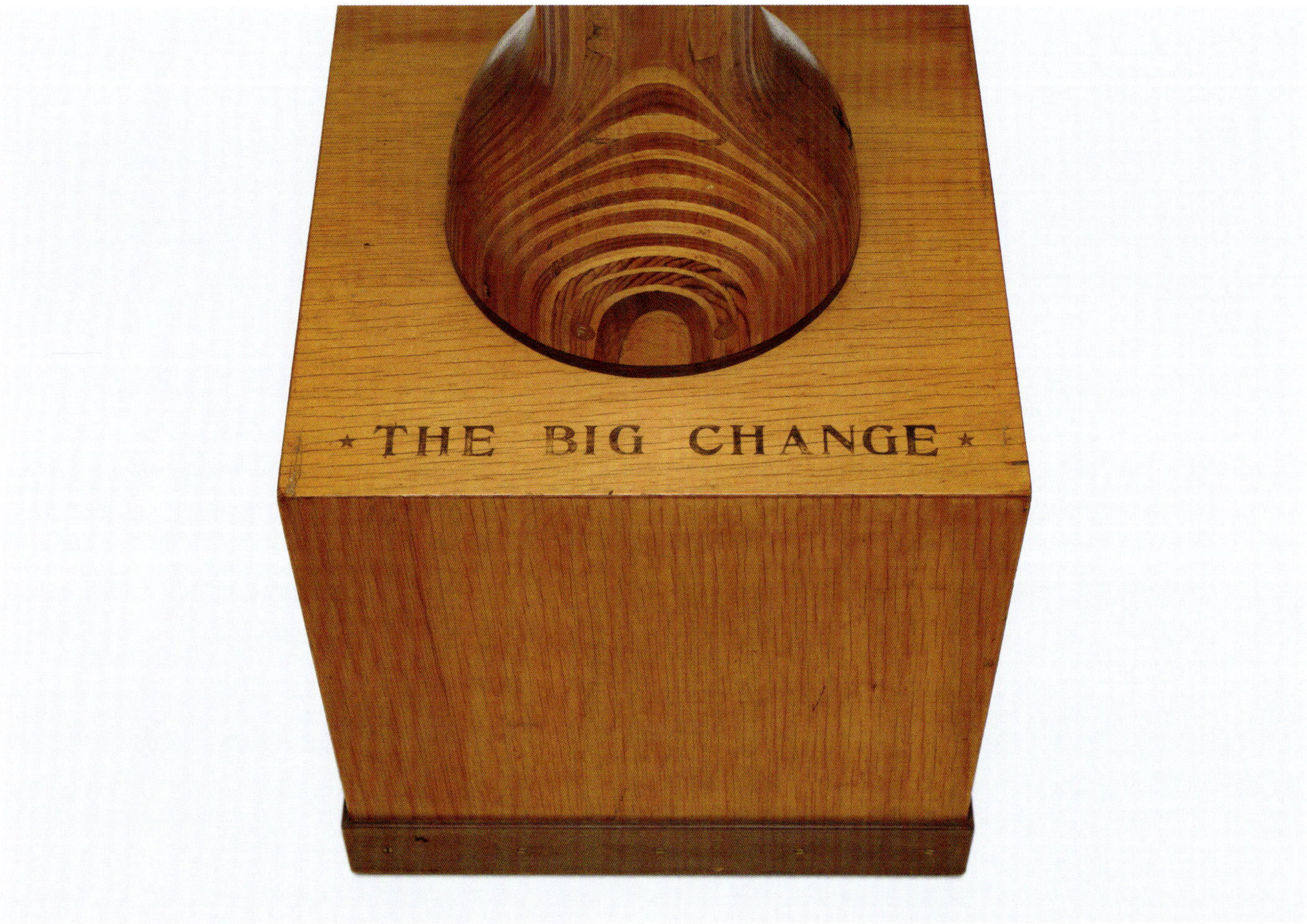

★ THE BIG CHANGE ★

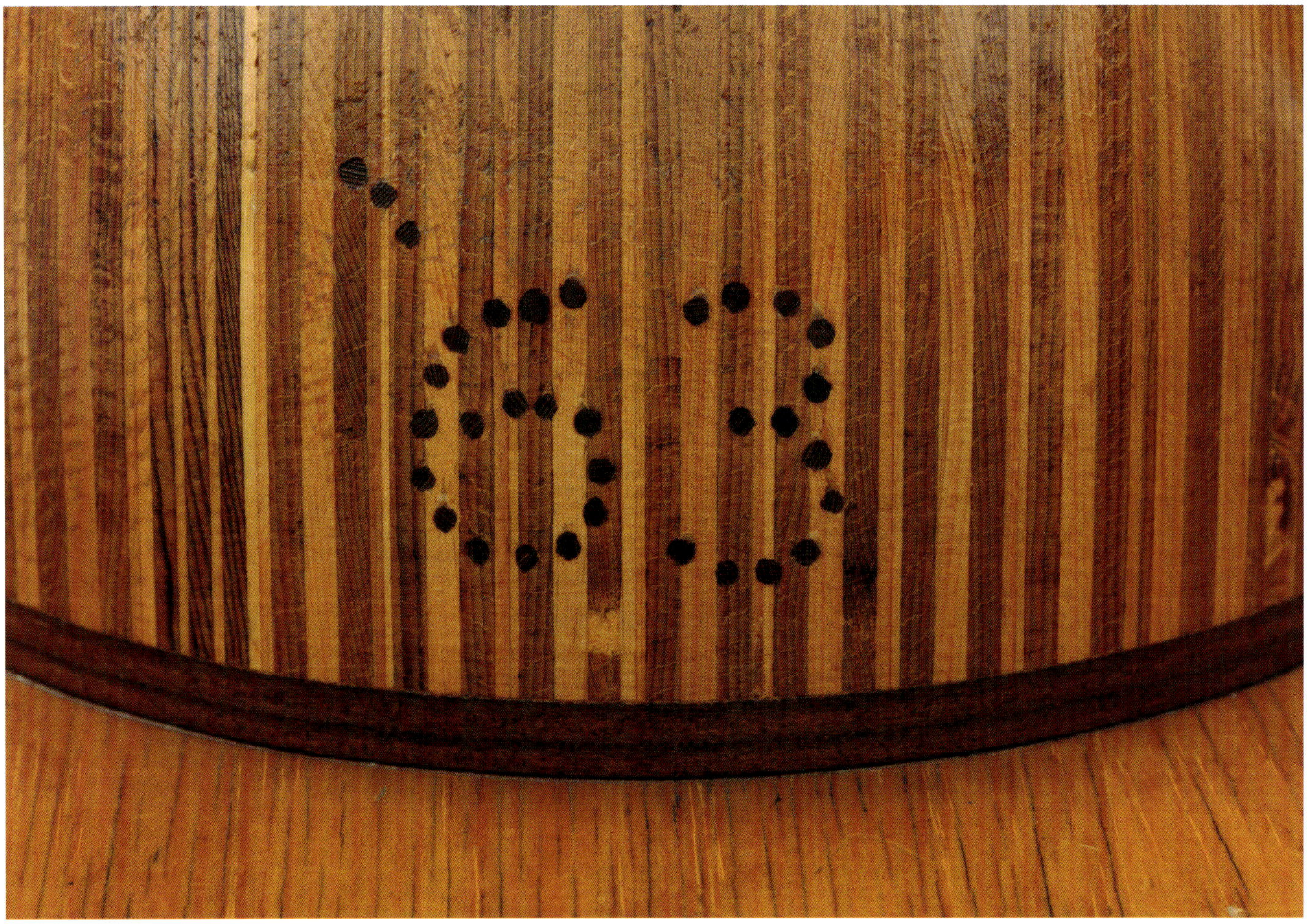

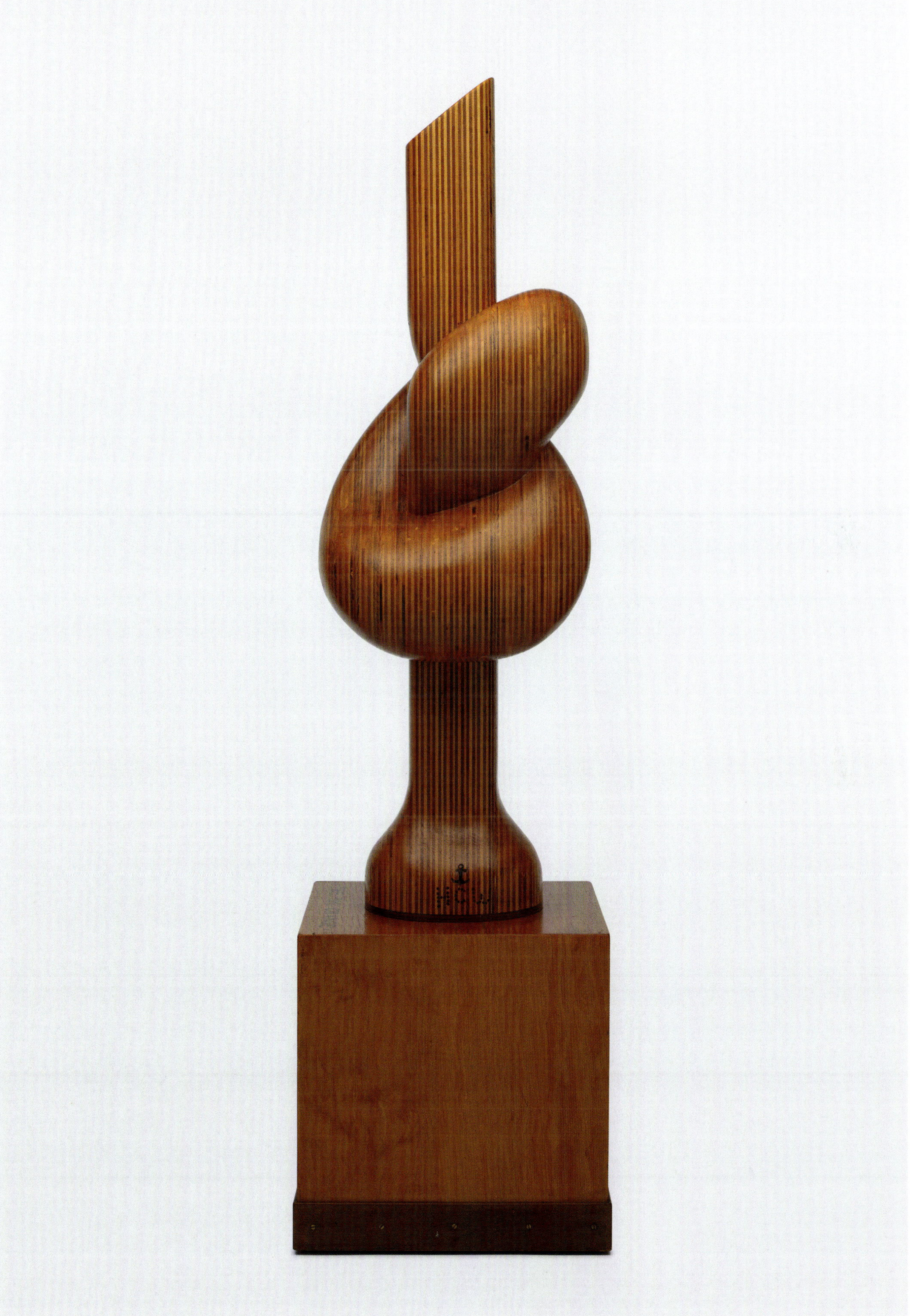

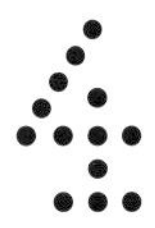

ECLIPSE #1

1963
PINE, PLATE-GLASS MIRROR,
PAINT, BRASS PLATE,
AND RUBBER BUMPERS

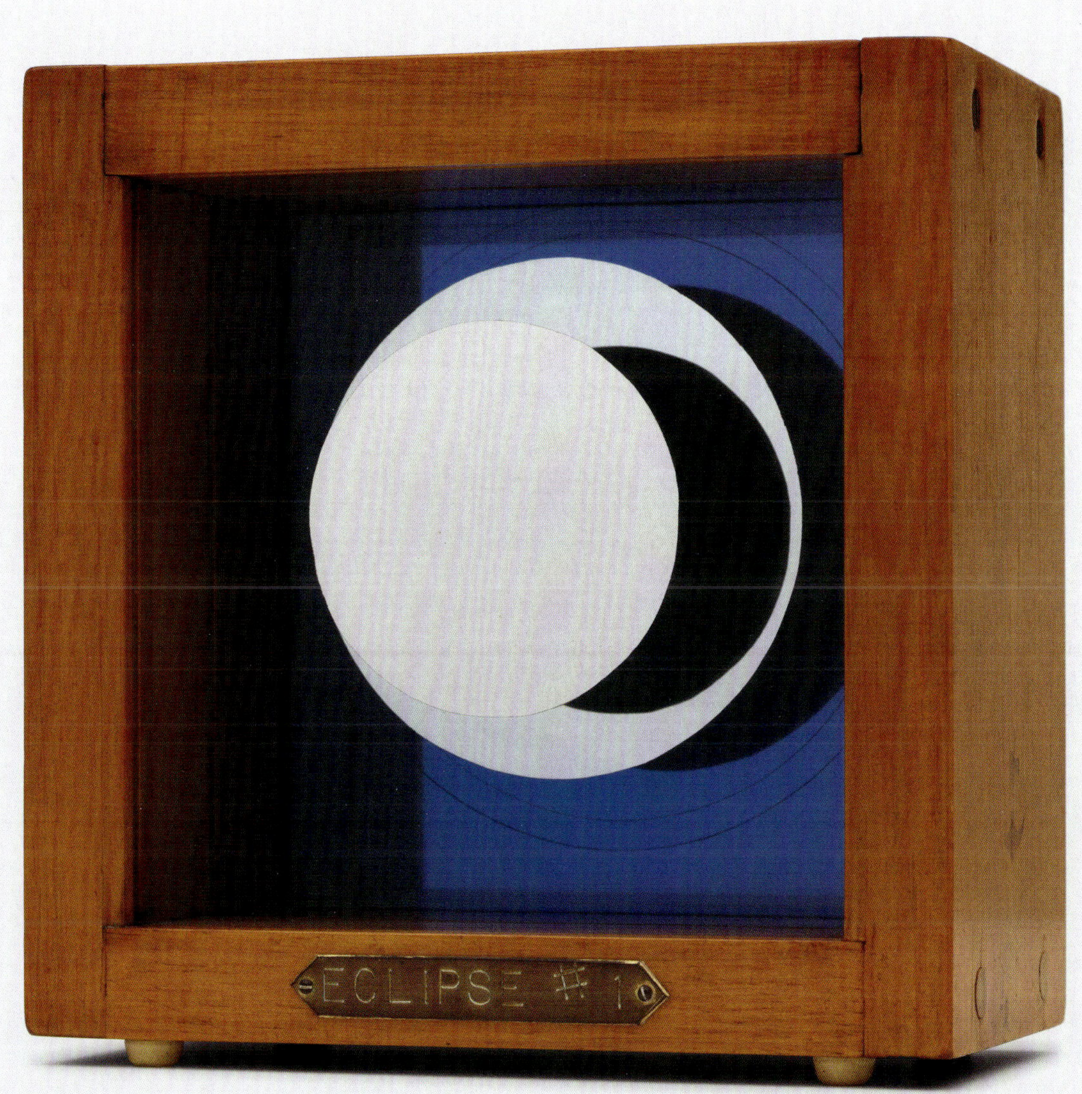
ECLIPSE # 1

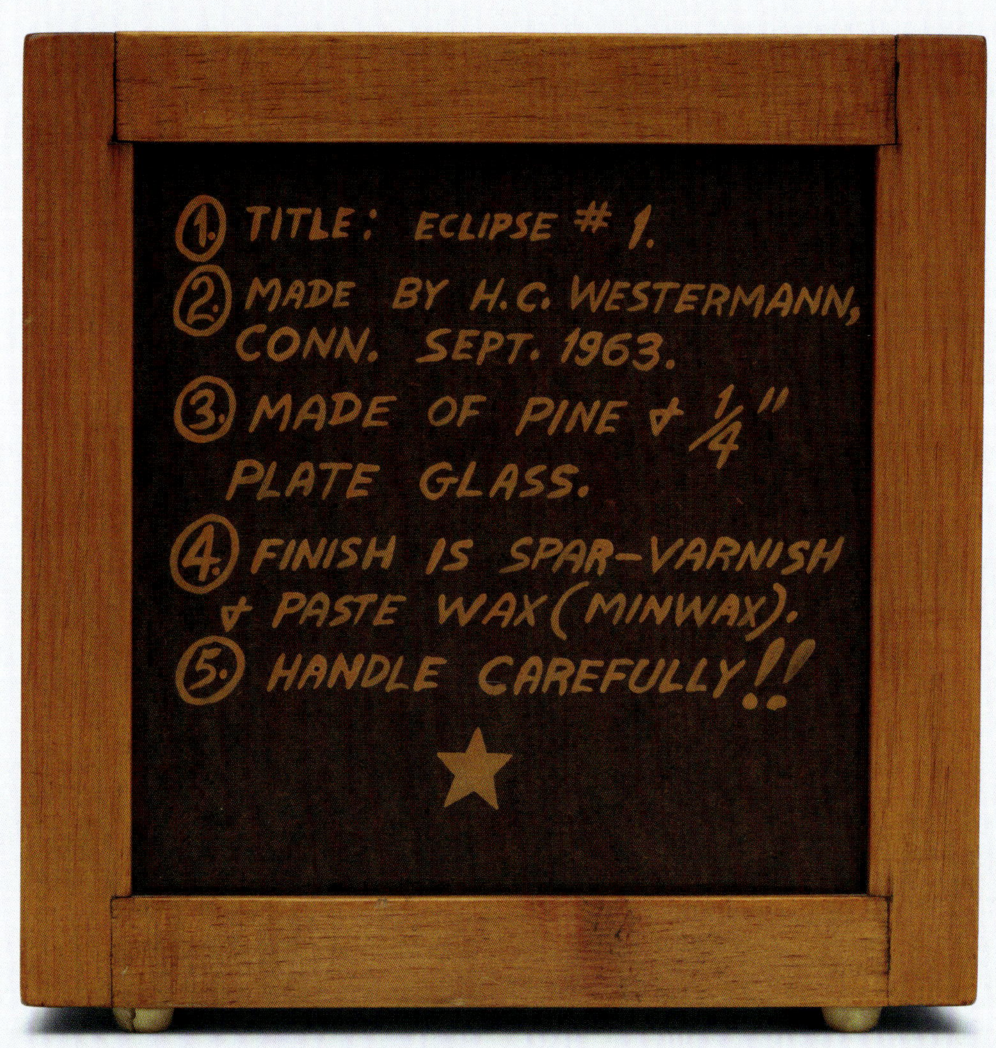

1. TITLE: ECLIPSE # 1.
2. MADE BY H.C. WESTERMANN, CONN. SEPT. 1963.
3. MADE OF PINE & 1/4" PLATE GLASS.
4. FINISH IS SPAR-VARNISH & PASTE WAX (MINWAX).
5. HANDLE CAREFULLY!!

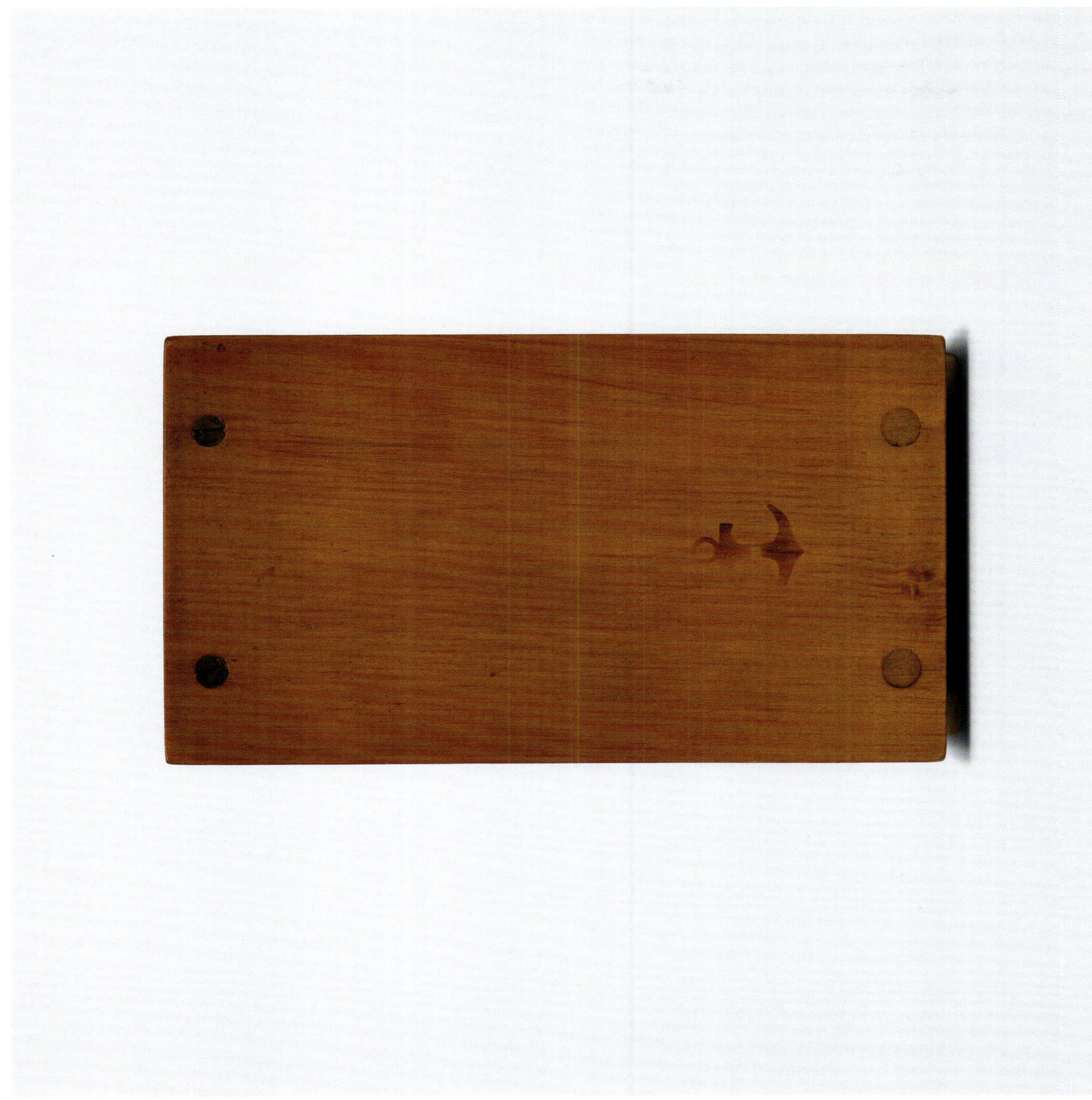

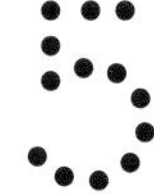

THE NIGHT LIFE

1963
PLATE-GLASS MIRROR, FIR,
MASONITE, BRASS PLATE,
RUBBER BUMPERS, AND INK

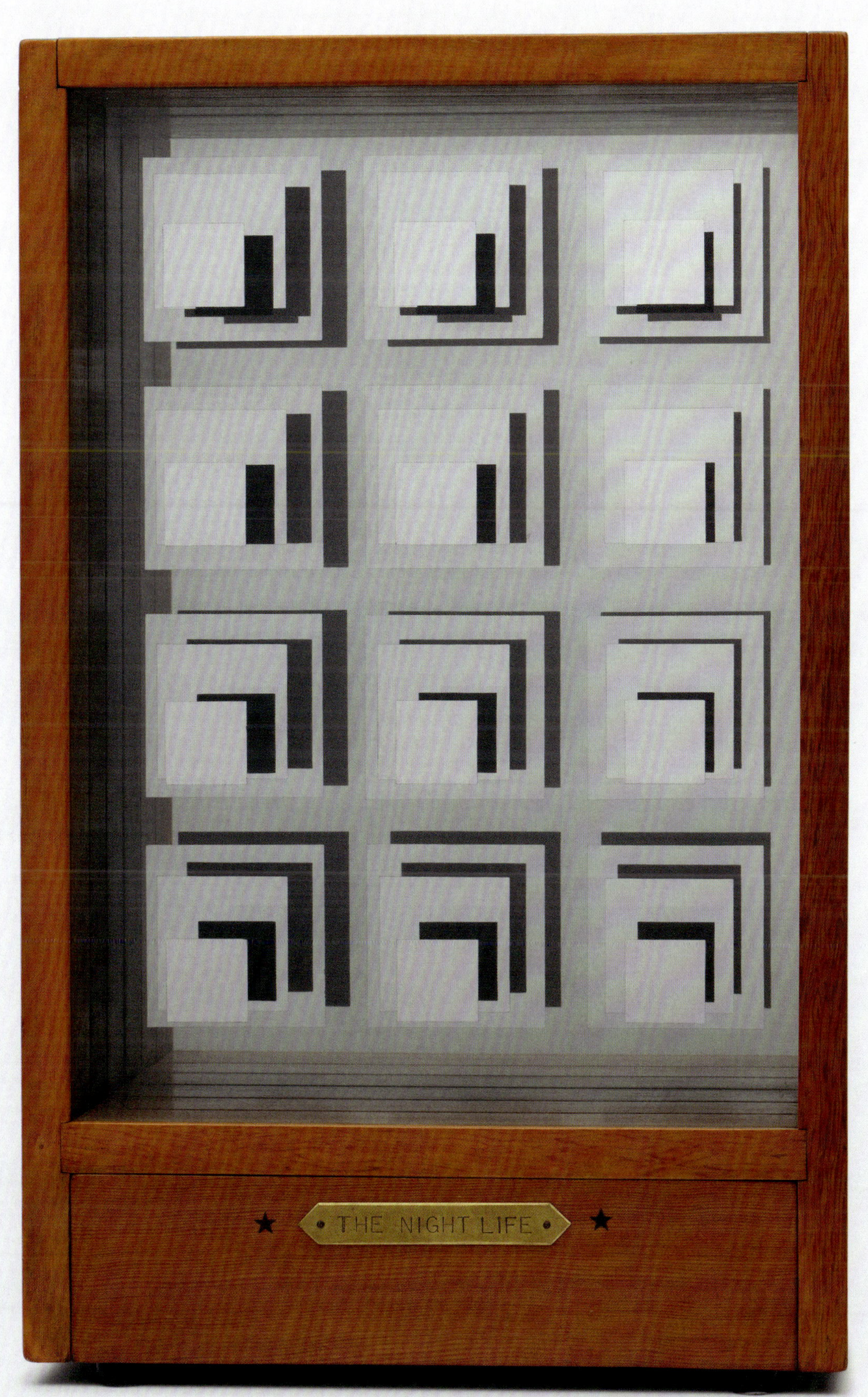

★ • THE NIGHT LIFE • ★

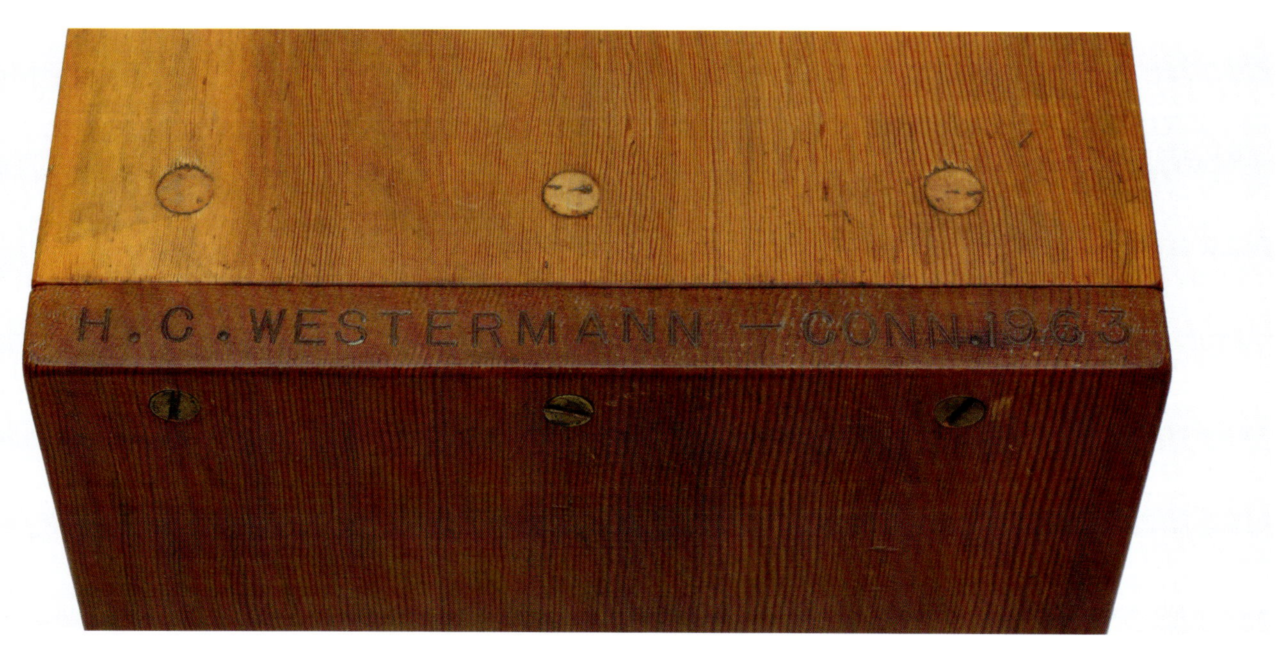
H.C.WESTERMANN — CONN.1963

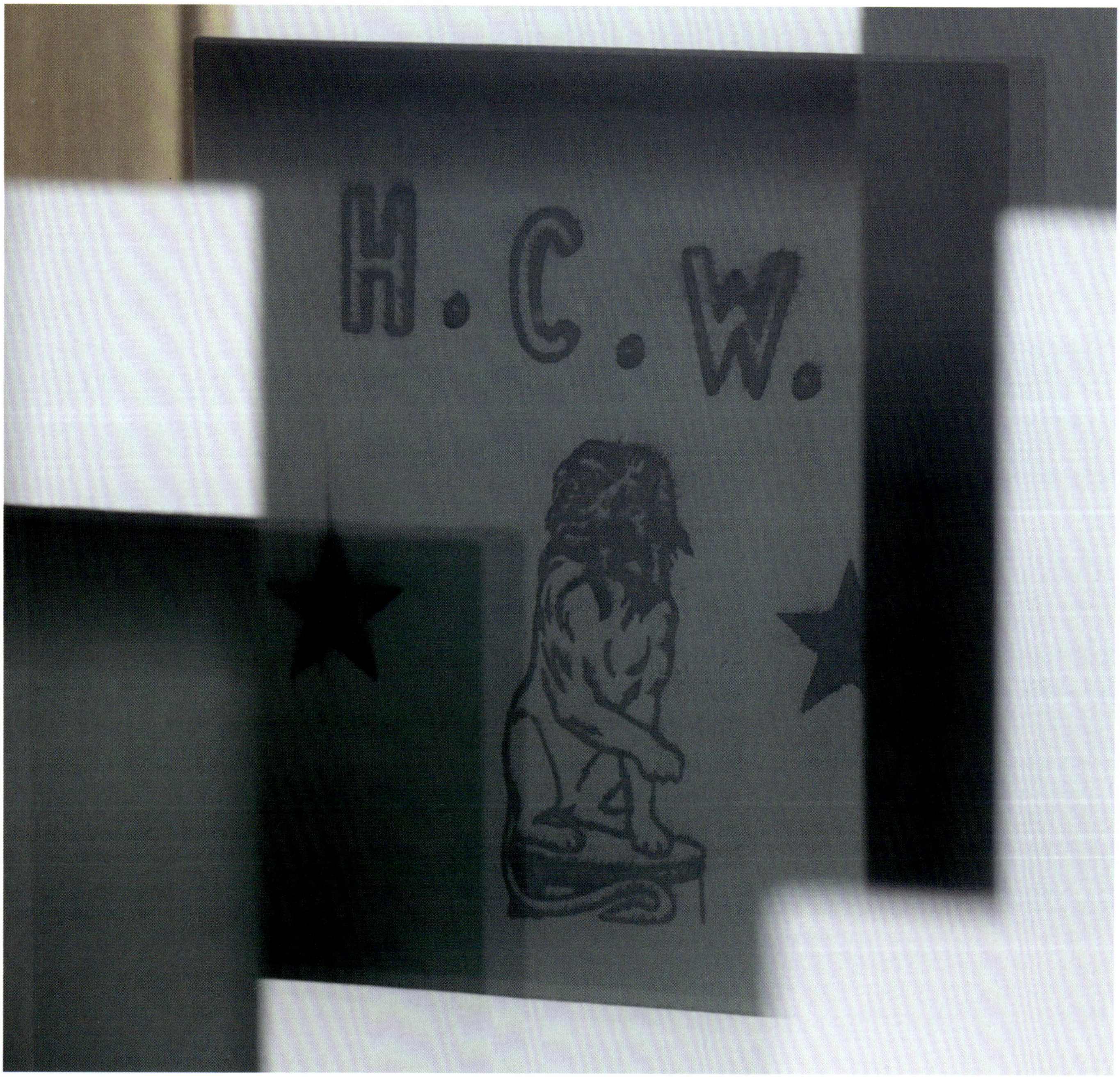

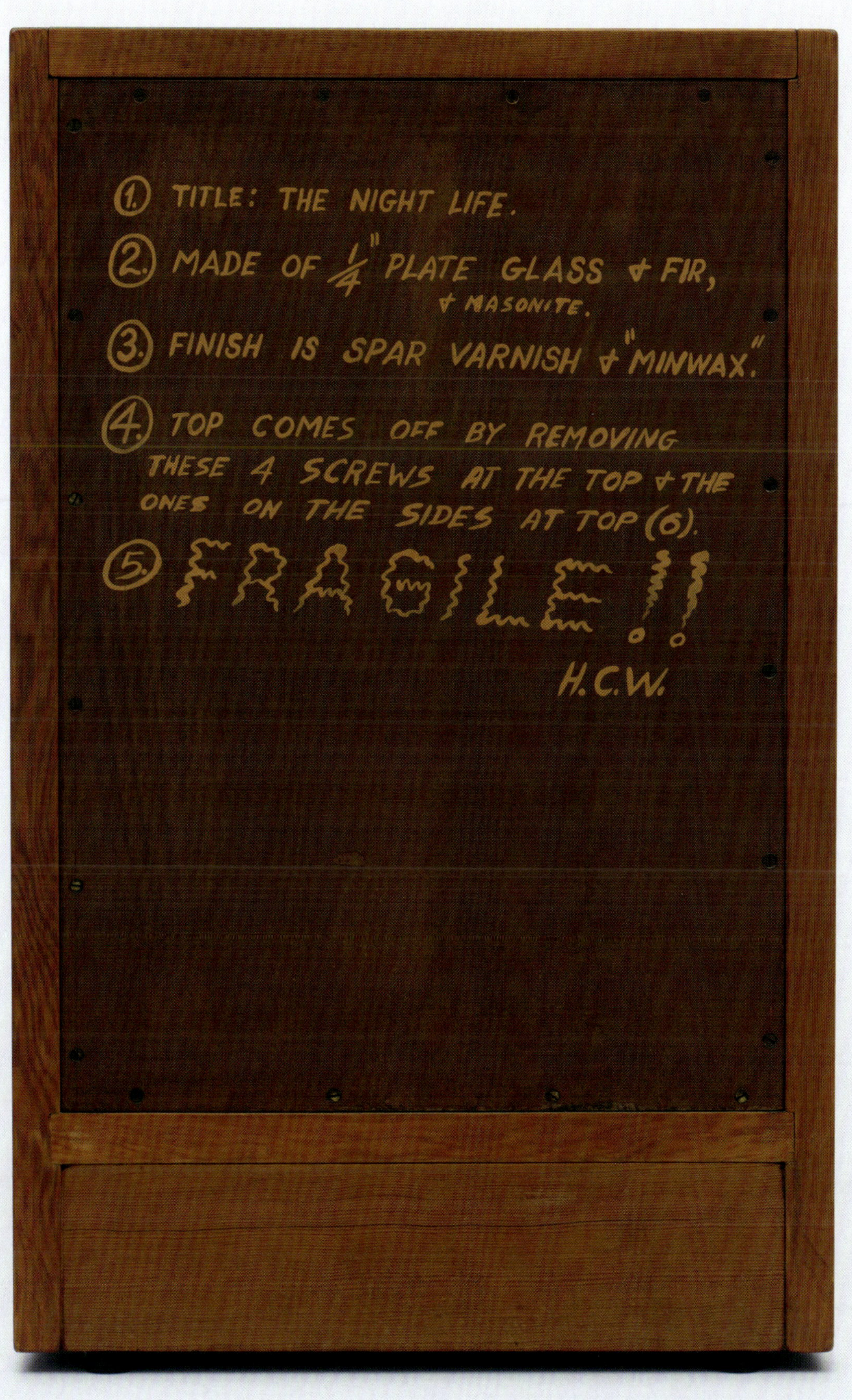
1. TITLE: THE NIGHT LIFE.
2. MADE OF 1/4" PLATE GLASS & FIR, & MASONITE.
3. FINISH IS SPAR VARNISH & "MINWAX."
4. TOP COMES OFF BY REMOVING THESE 4 SCREWS AT THE TOP & THE ONES ON THE SIDES AT TOP (6).
5. FRAGILE!!
H.C.W.

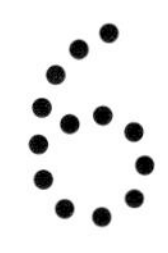

THE SONIC BOOM

1963
WOOD, PLATE-GLASS MIRROR,
BUBINGA, PAINT, AND INK

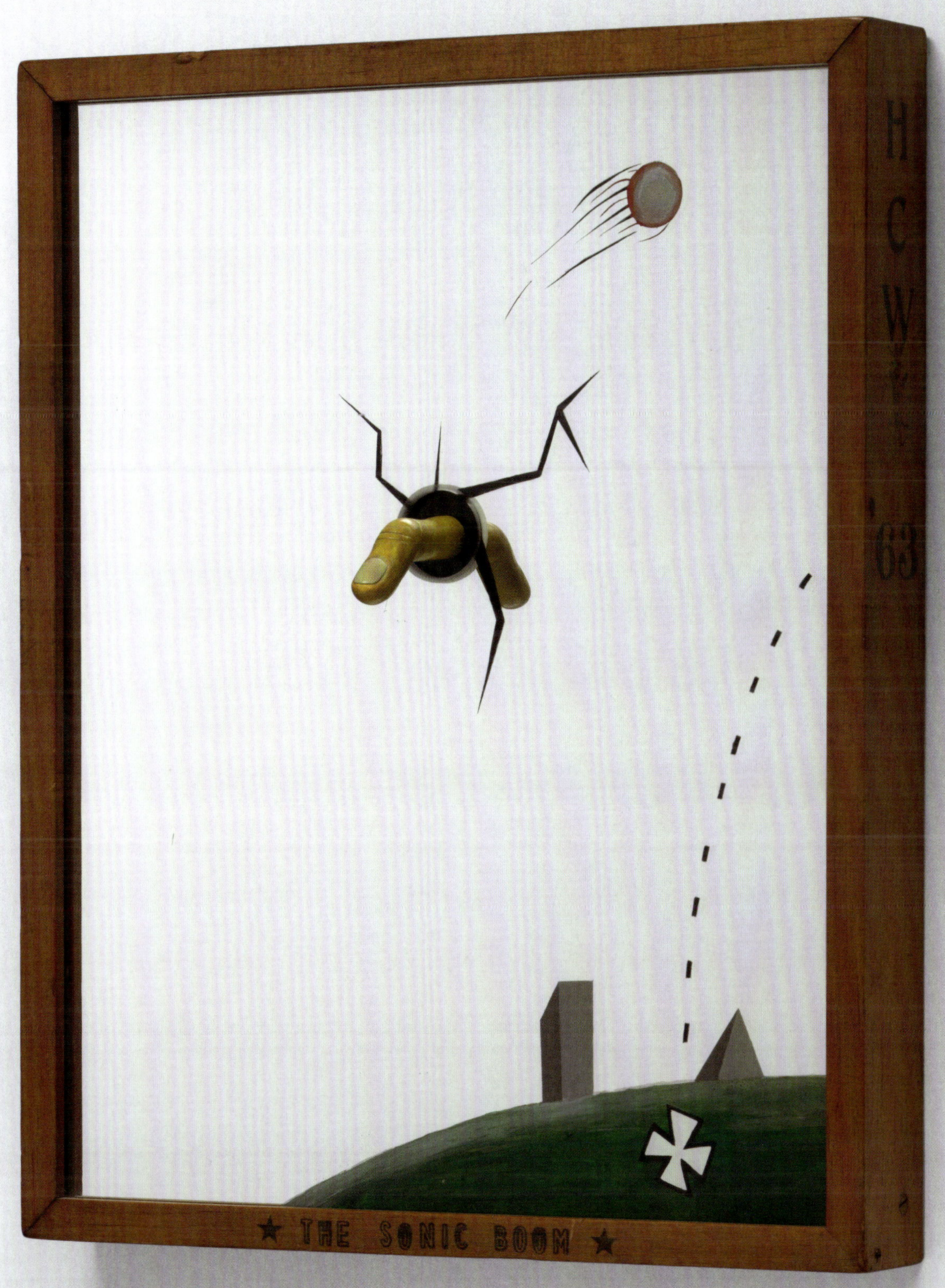

THE SONIC BOOM

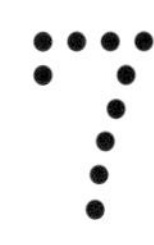

HOMAGE TO
AMERICAN ART
(DEDICATED
TO ELIE NADELMAN)

1988
DOUGLAS FIR, ASH, CAST LEAD,
AND ANTIQUE SHOVEL HANDLE

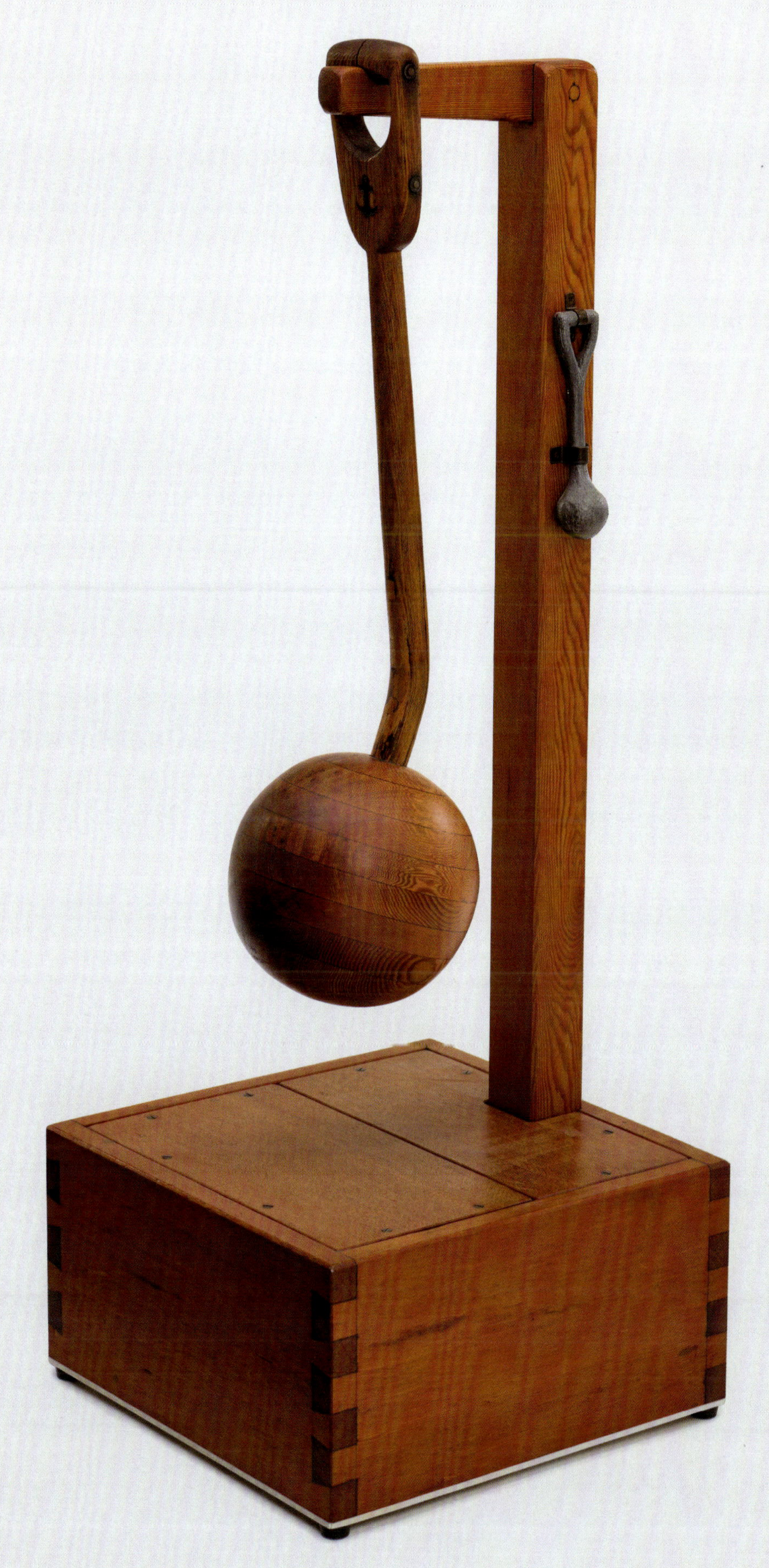

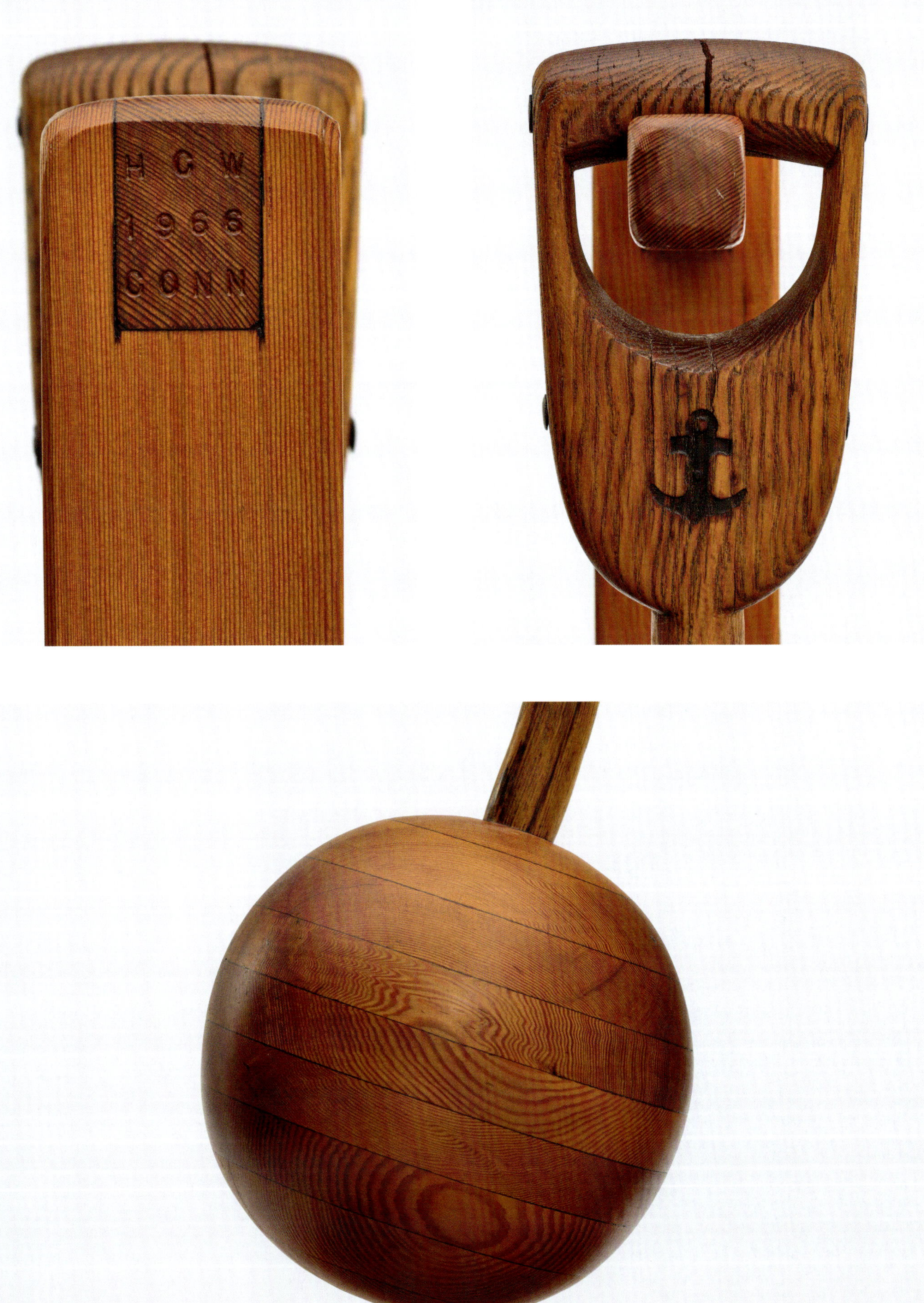

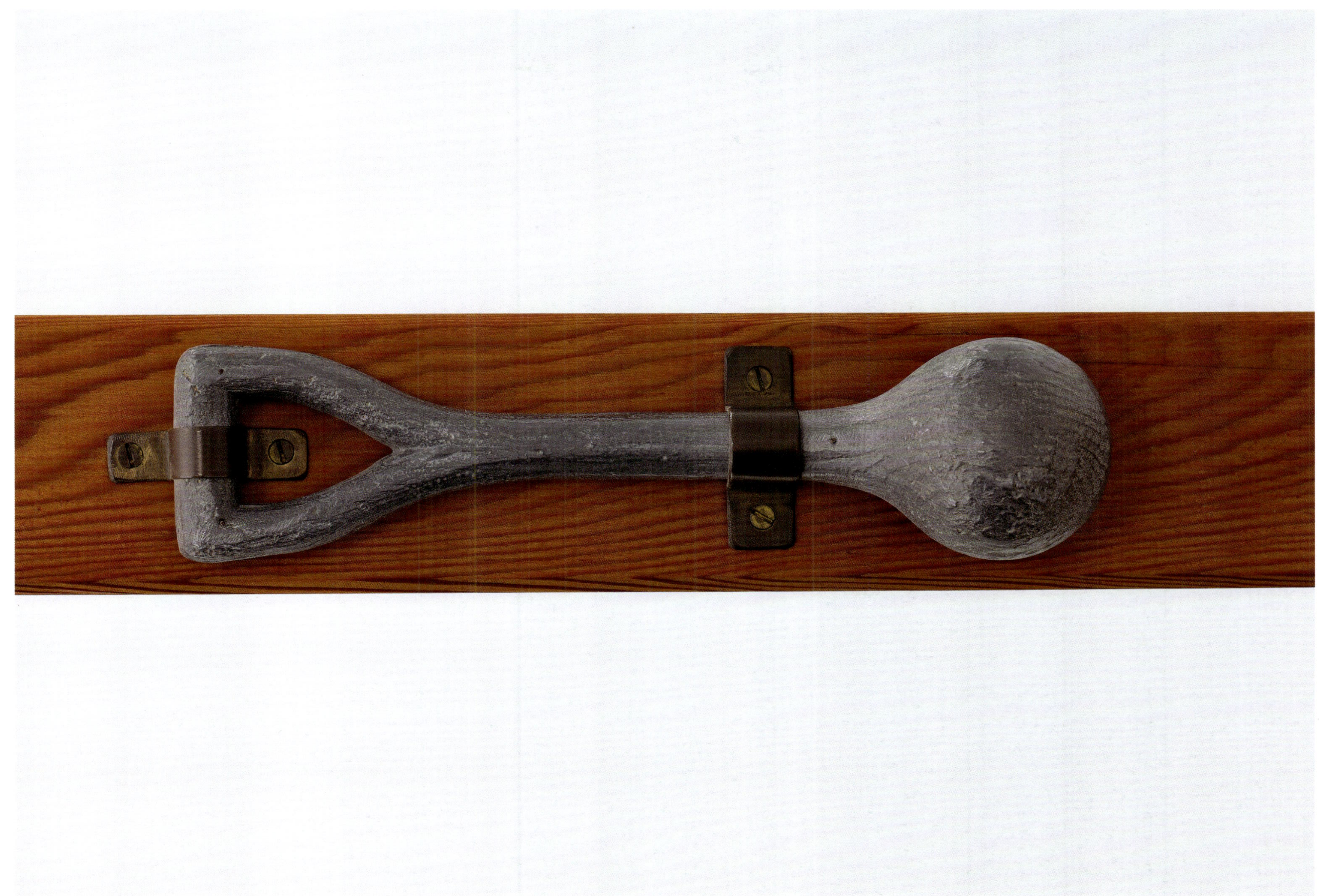

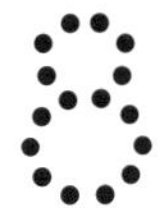

ROTTING JET WING

1966
PINE, PLATE GLASS, FELT,
AND COPPER

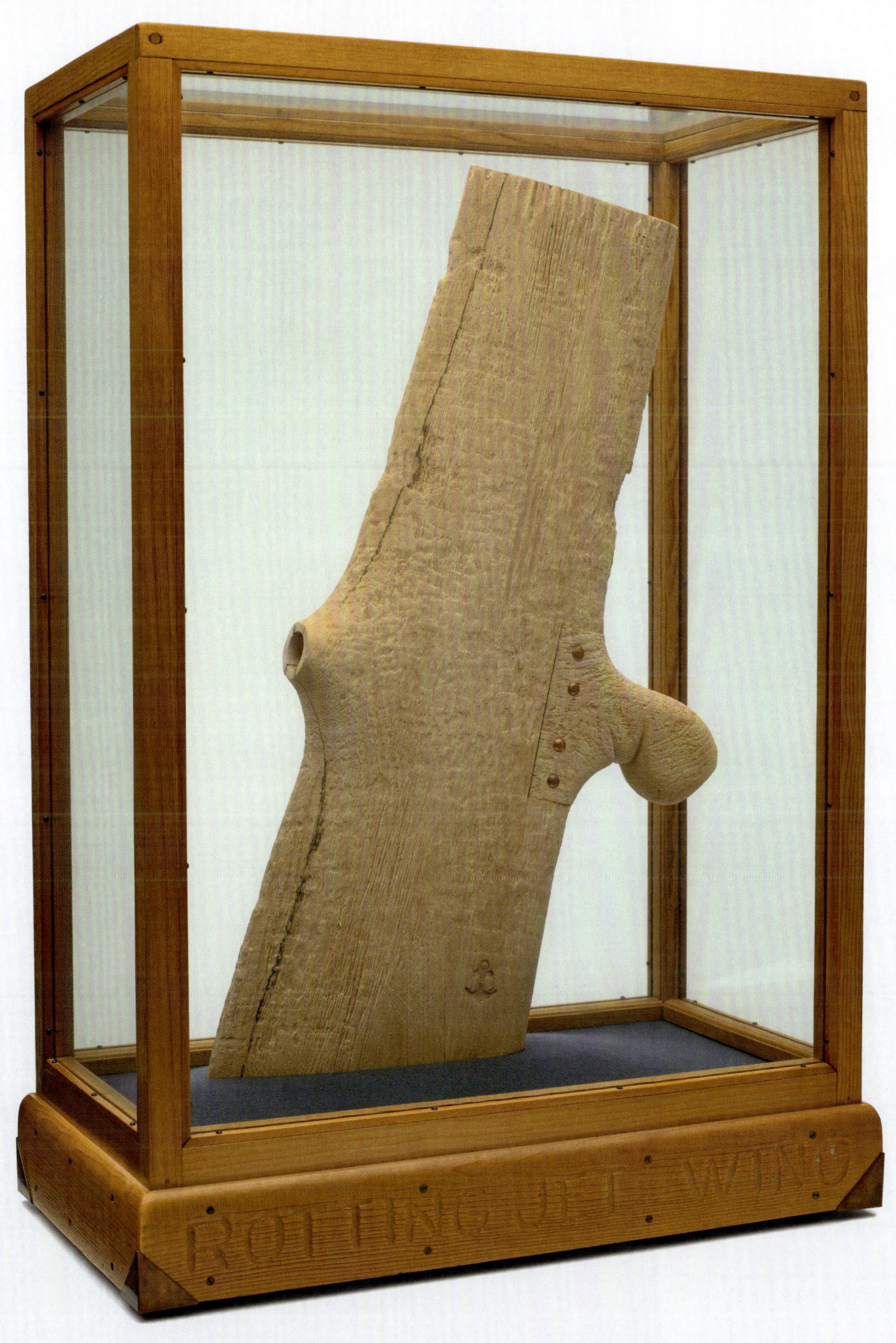

ROLLING JET WING

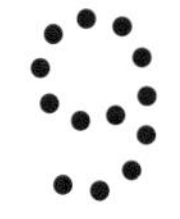

WORLD'S
STRONGEST GLUE

1966
SOLID CAST BRONZE, BRASS,
AND PAINT

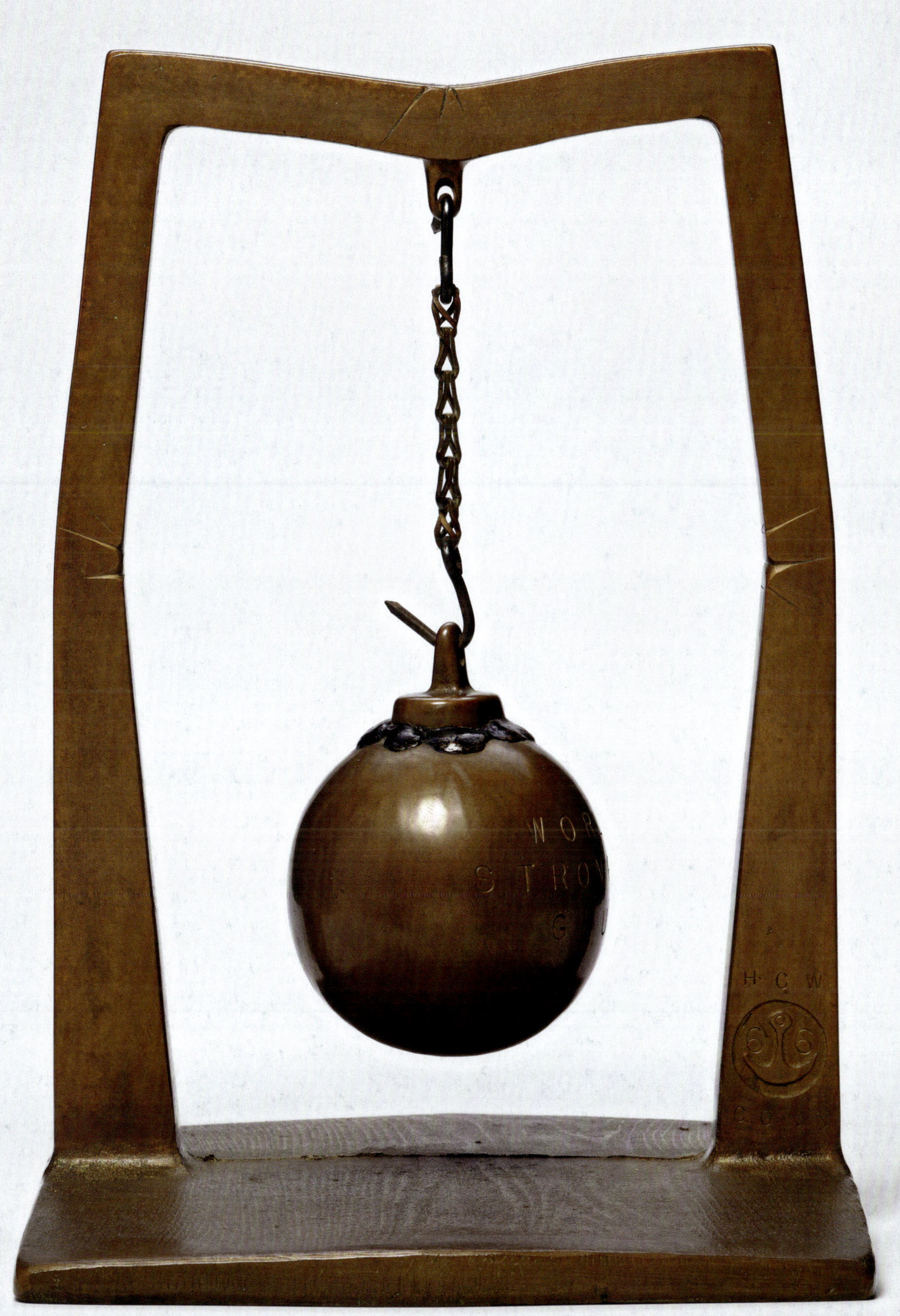

WOR
STRO
G
H C W
CO

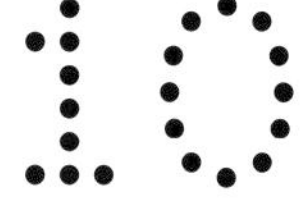

CONTROL

1968
OAK, MAHOGANY, PINE, PLATE GLASS, TAR,
CHICKEN FEATHERS, SHEET COPPER,
BRASS, AND SOLDER

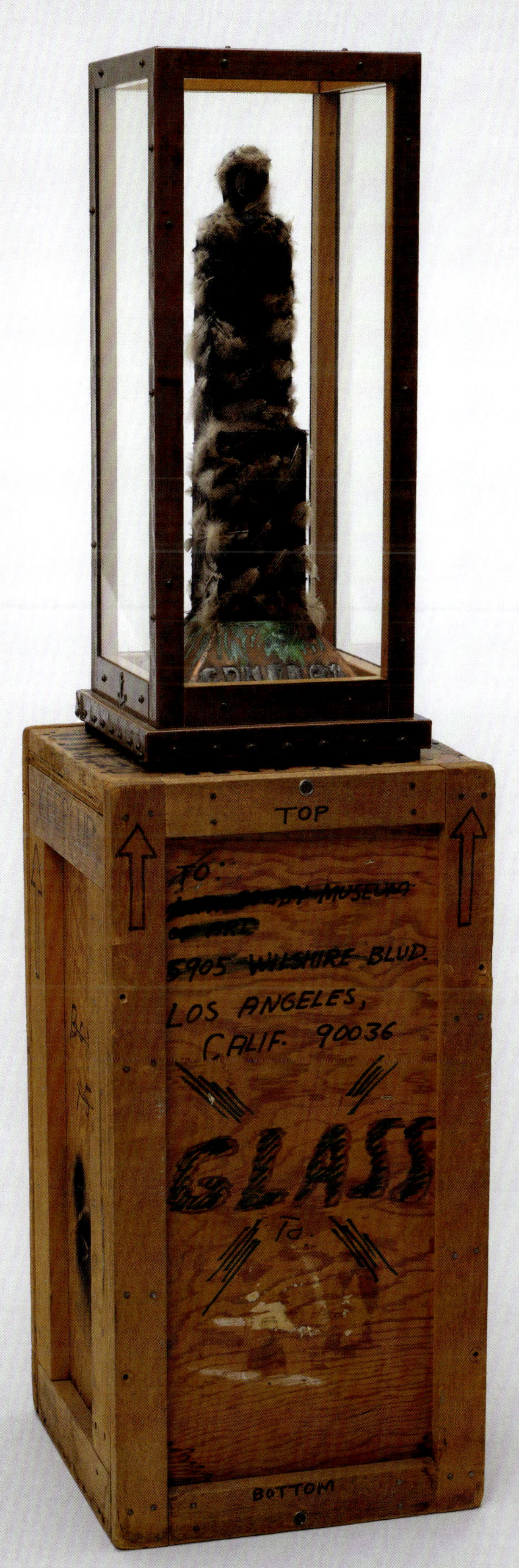
TOP
TO:
MUSEUM
5905 WILSHIRE BLVD.
LOS ANGELES,
CALIF. 90036
GLASS
TO
BOTTOM

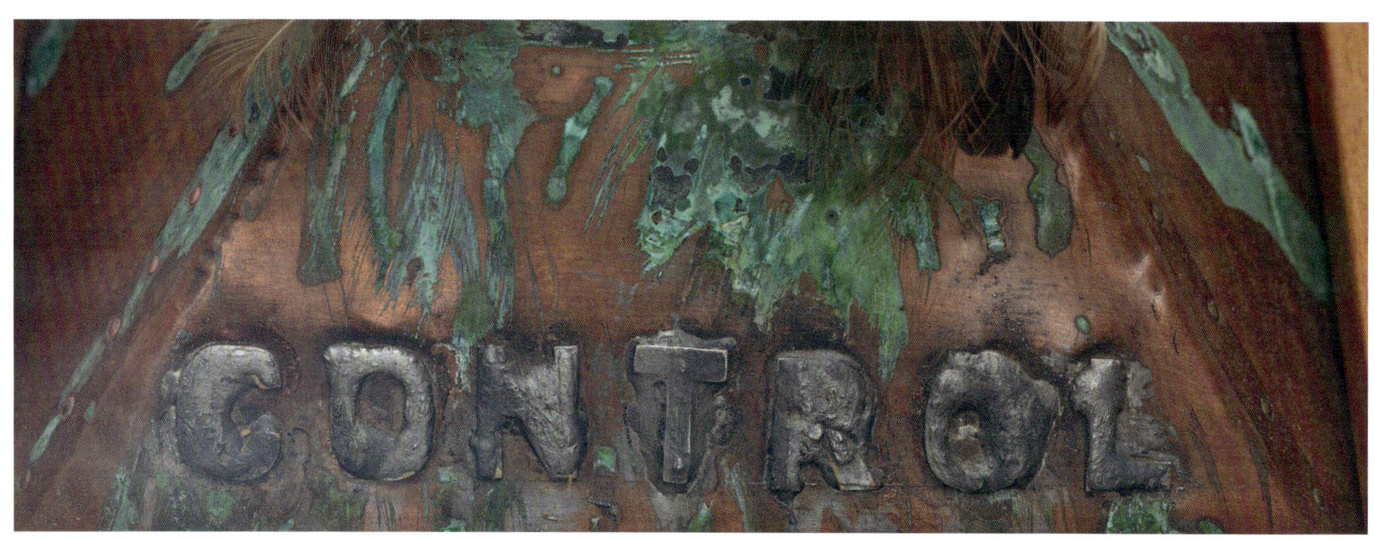

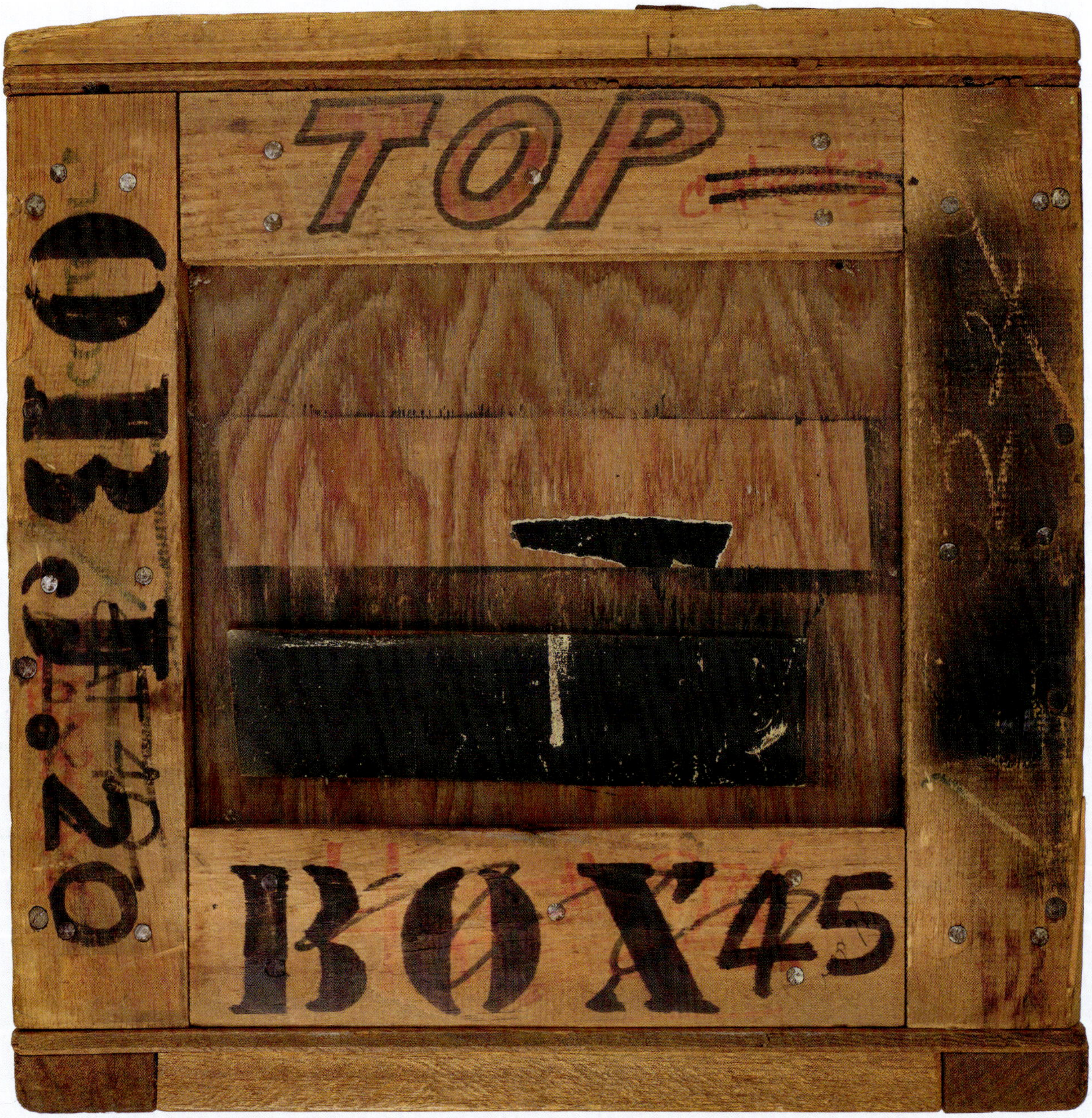

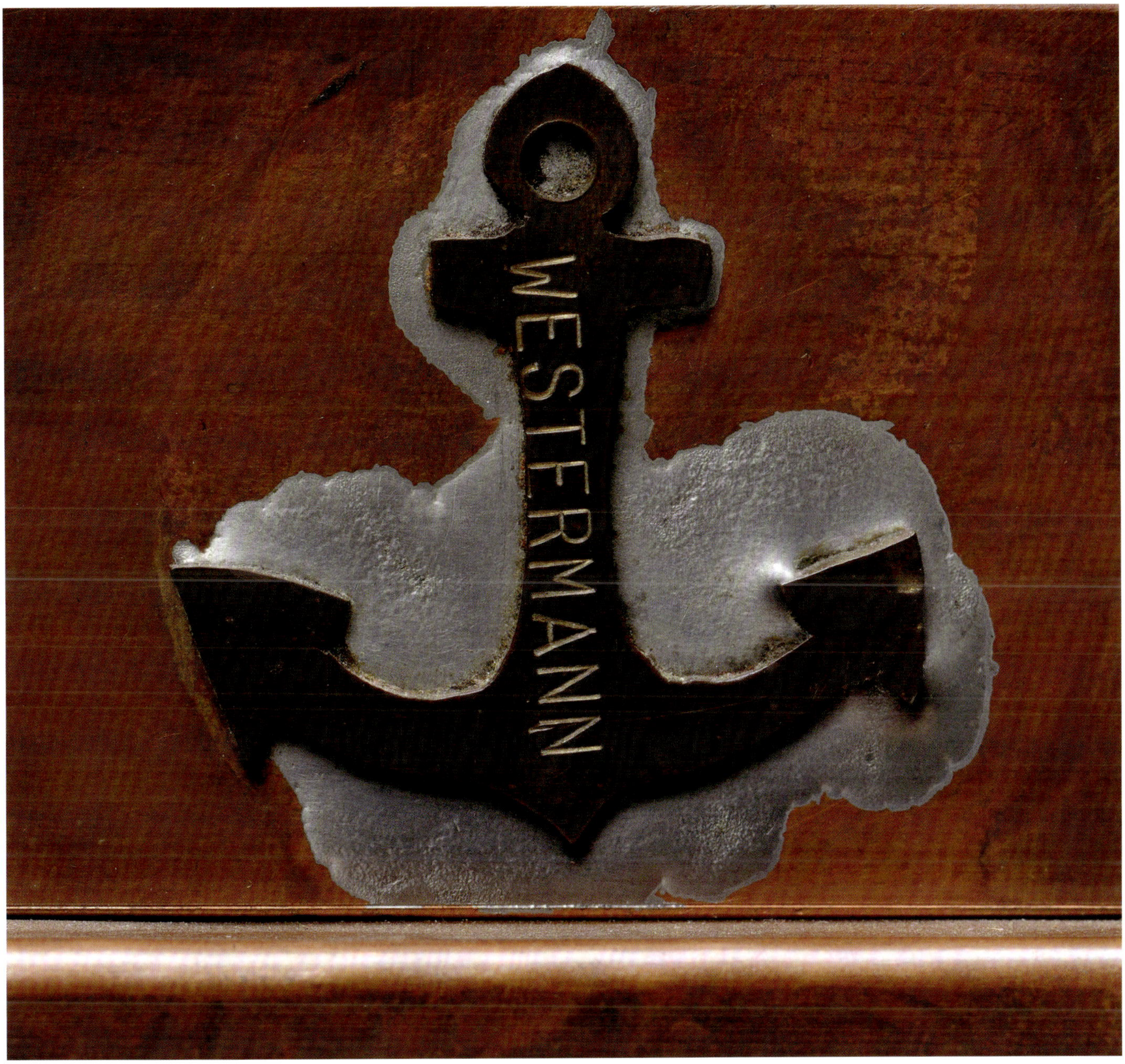

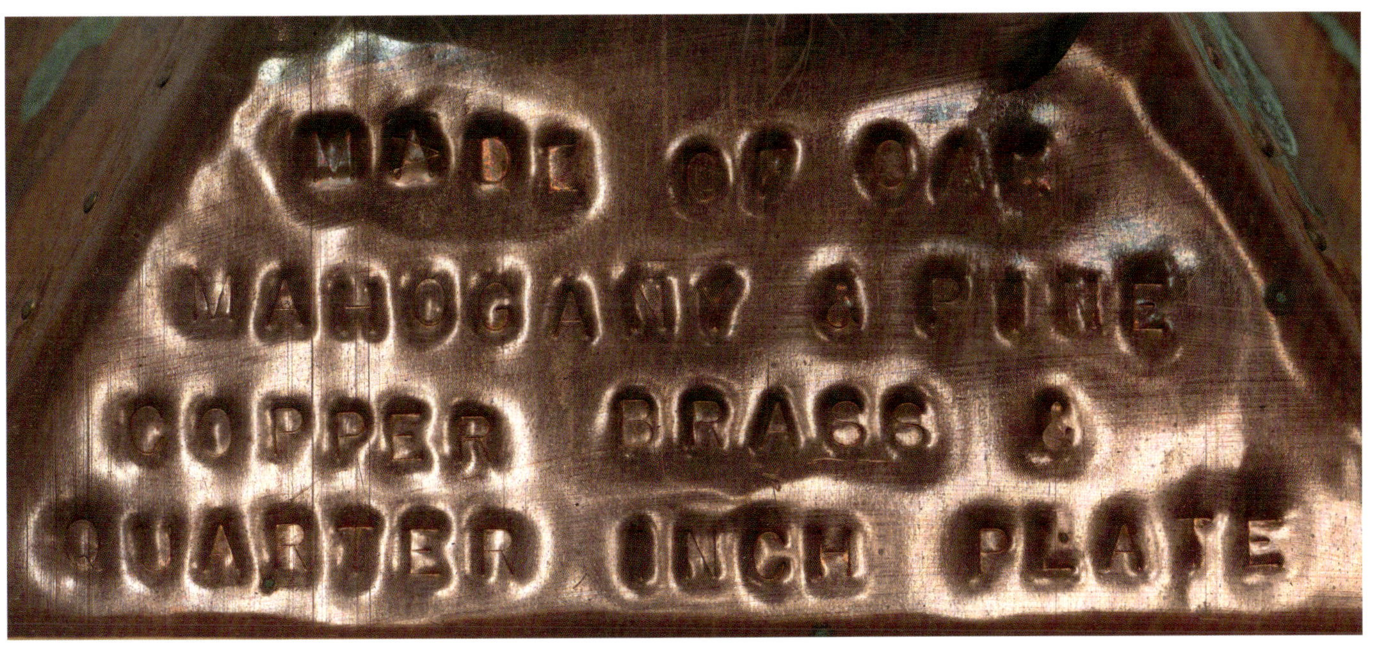
WESTERMANN
MADE OF OAK
MAHOGANY & PINE
COPPER BRASS &
QUARTER INCH PLATE

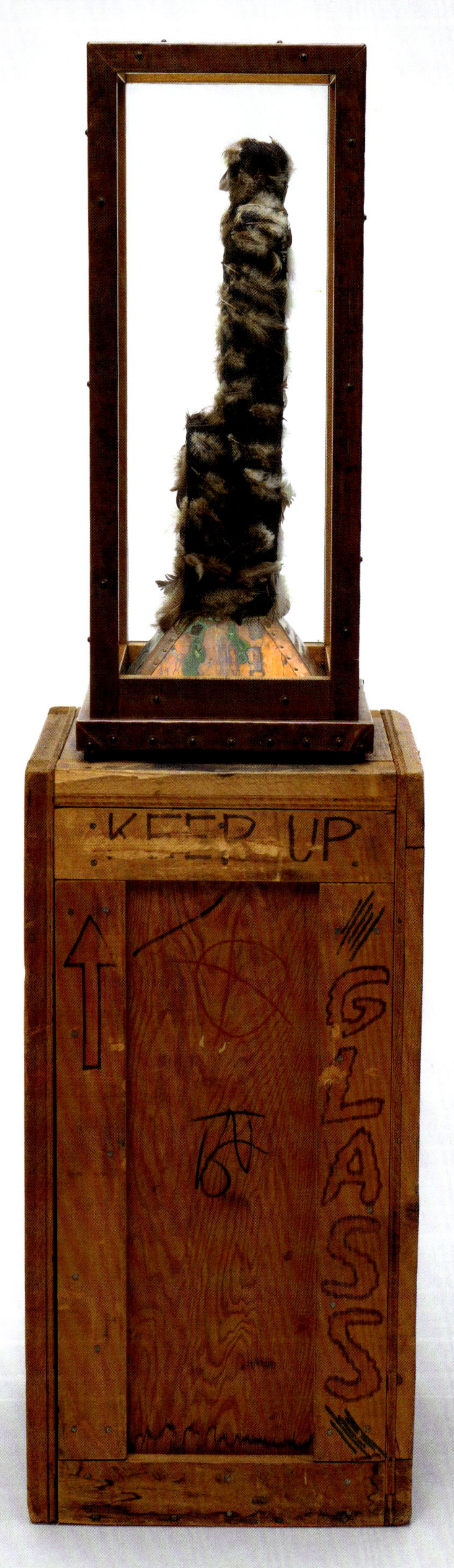
KEEP UP
GLASS

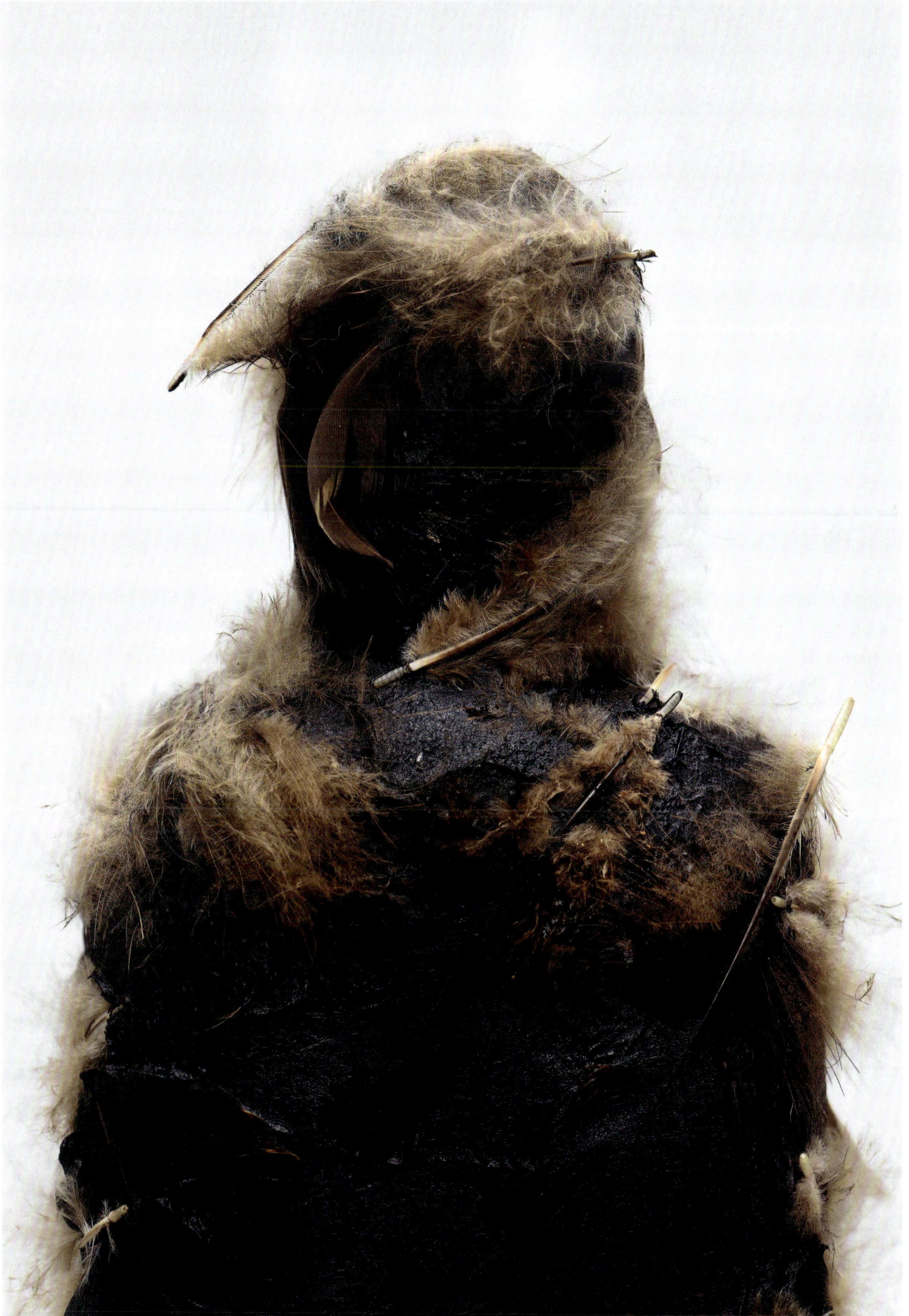

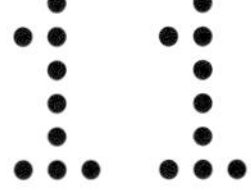

WET FLOWER

1968
WOOD, GLASS, CONNECTICUT
FIELDSTONE, LINOLEUM, DRIED ROOTS,
PUTTY, AND VARNISH

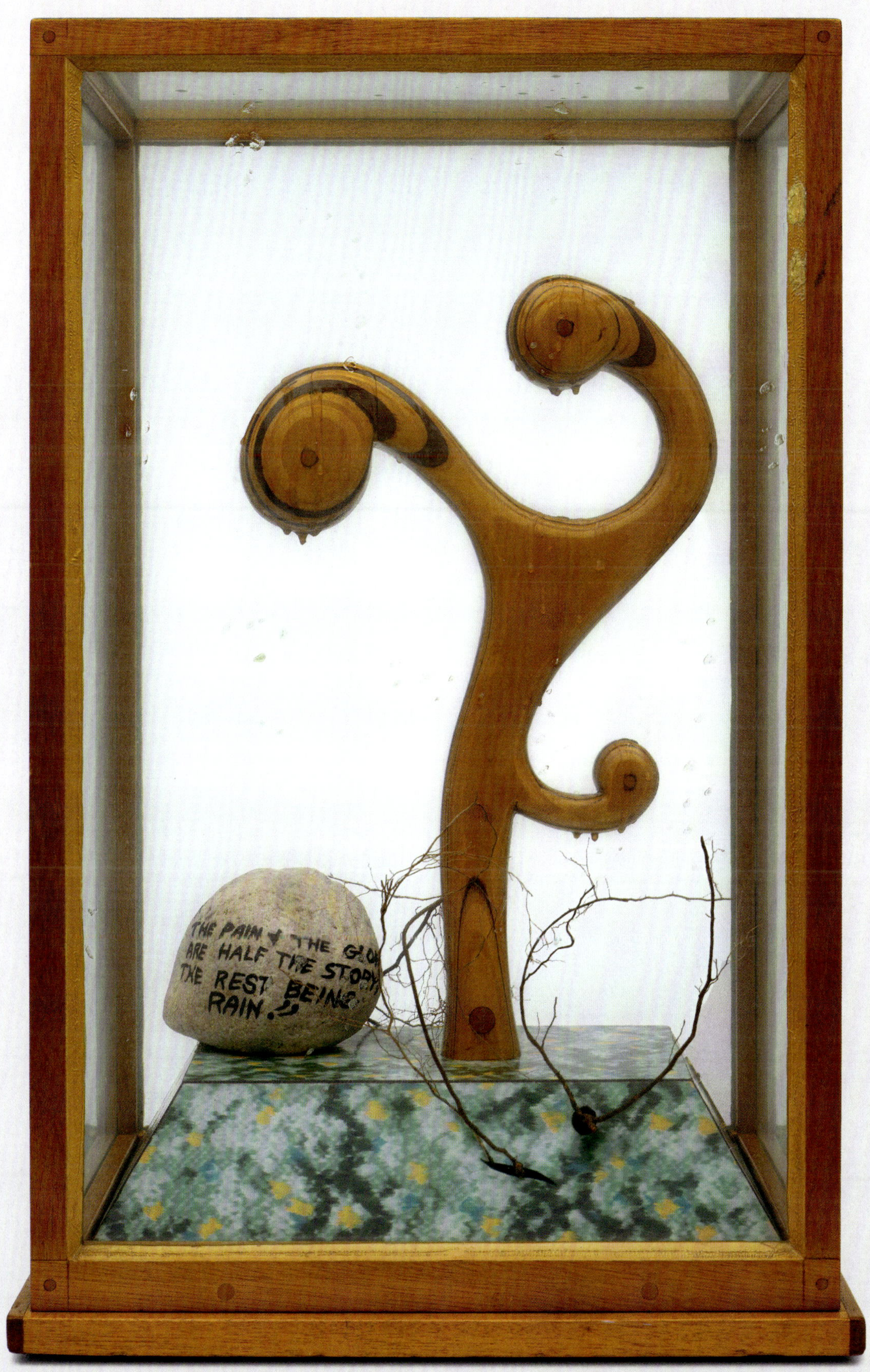

THE PAIN & THE GLORY
ARE HALF THE STORY
THE REST BEING
RAIN.

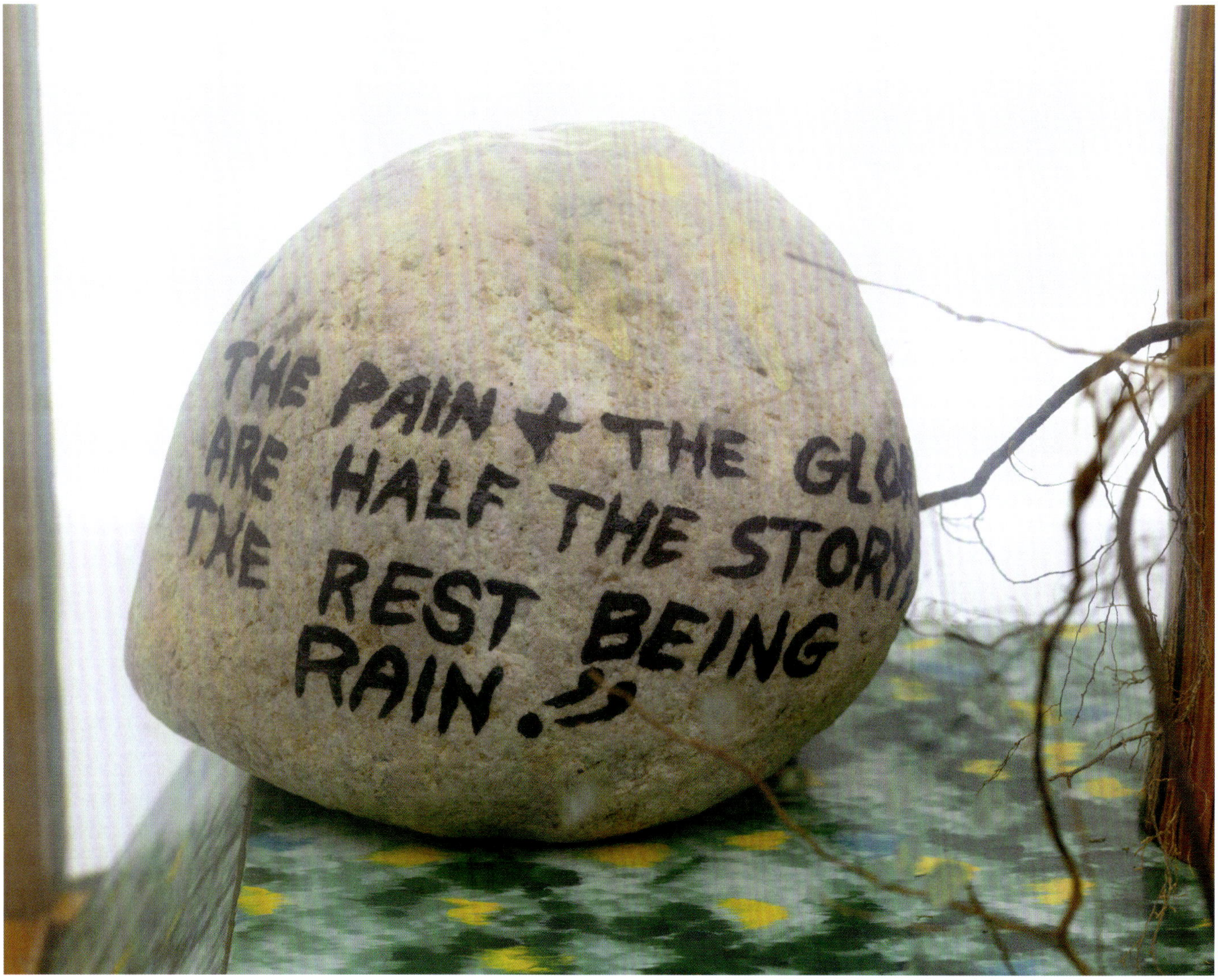

THE PAIN ✦ THE GLOR
ARE HALF THE STORY
THE REST BEING
RAIN. ♪

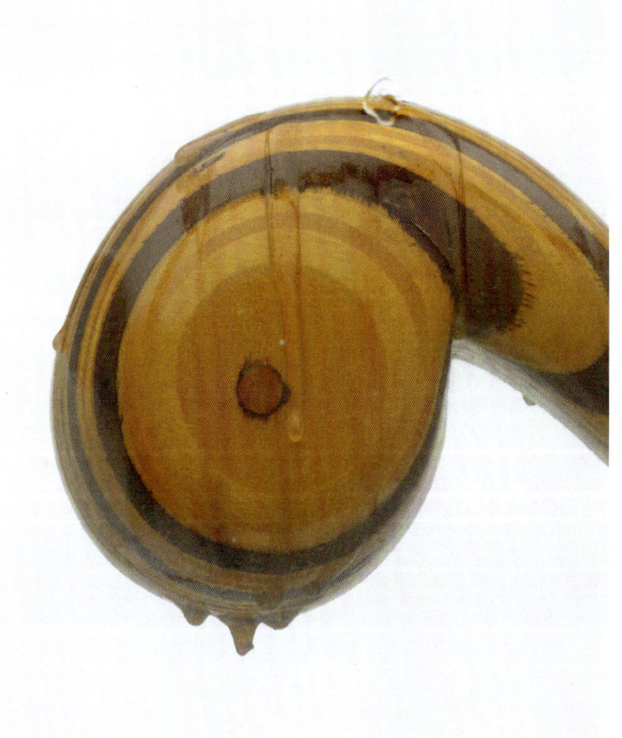

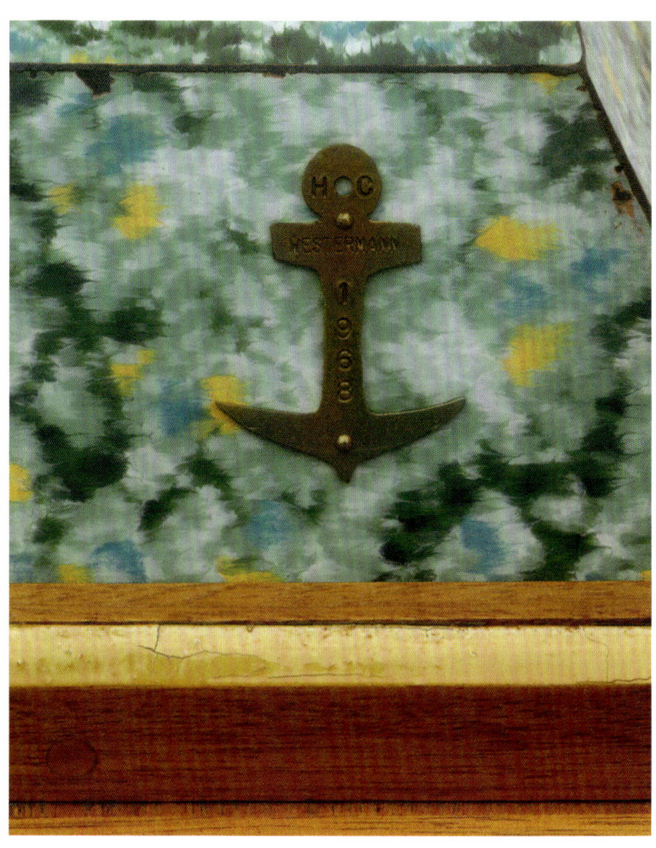
H C
WESTERMANN
1968

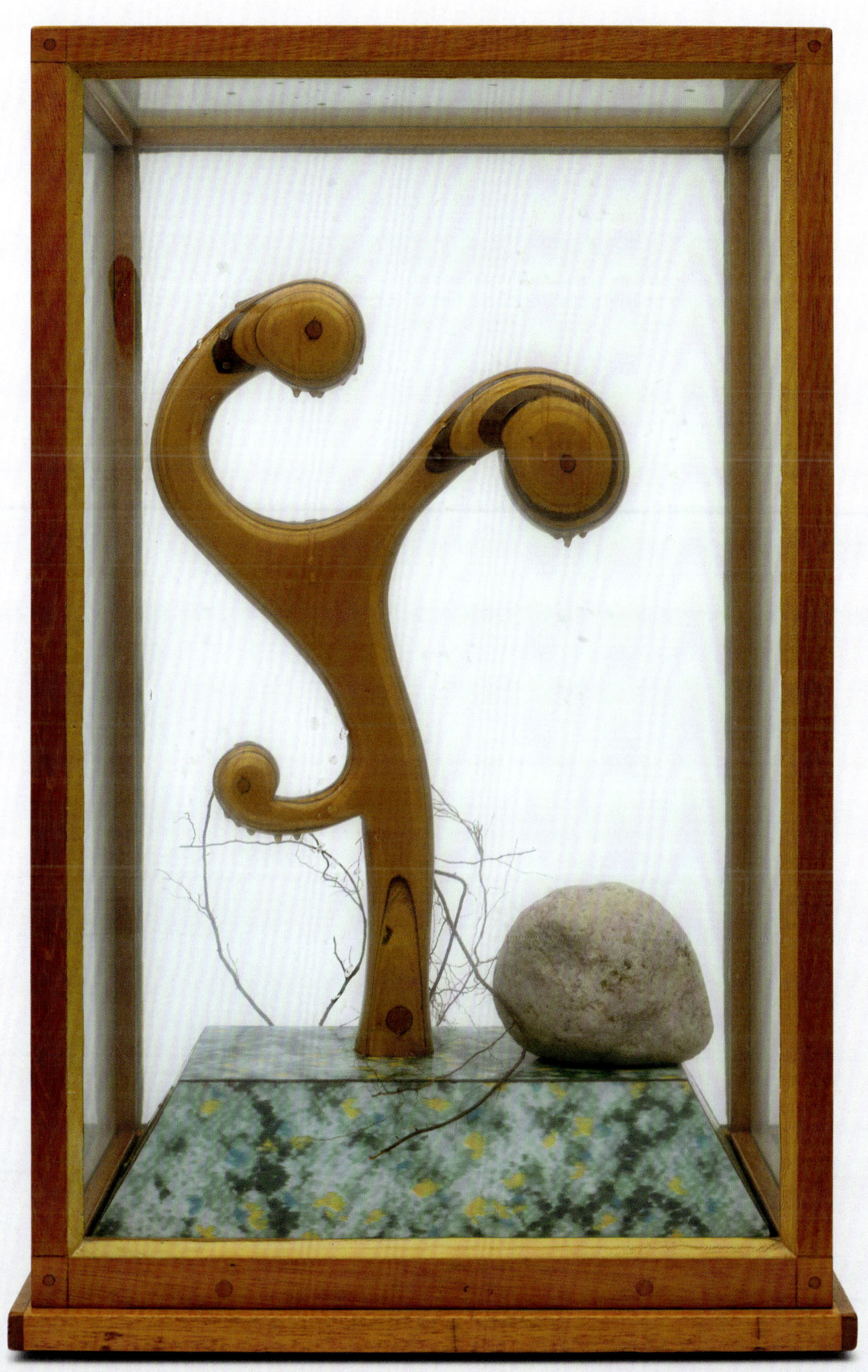

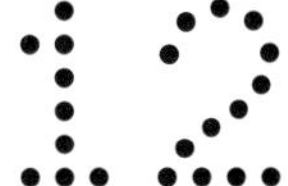

LITTLE EGYPT

1969
DOUGLAS FIR, PINE, OAK,
AND BRONZE

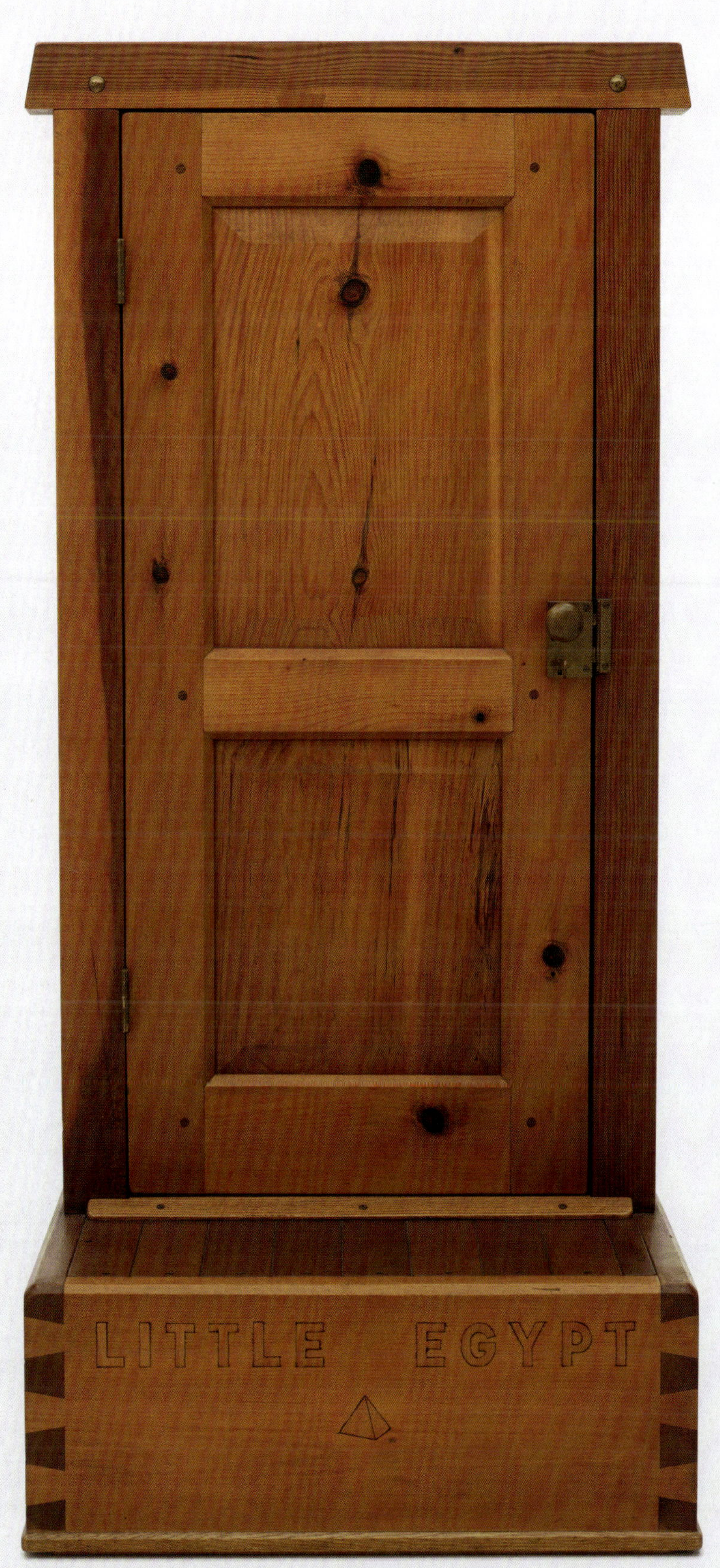

LITTLE EGYPT

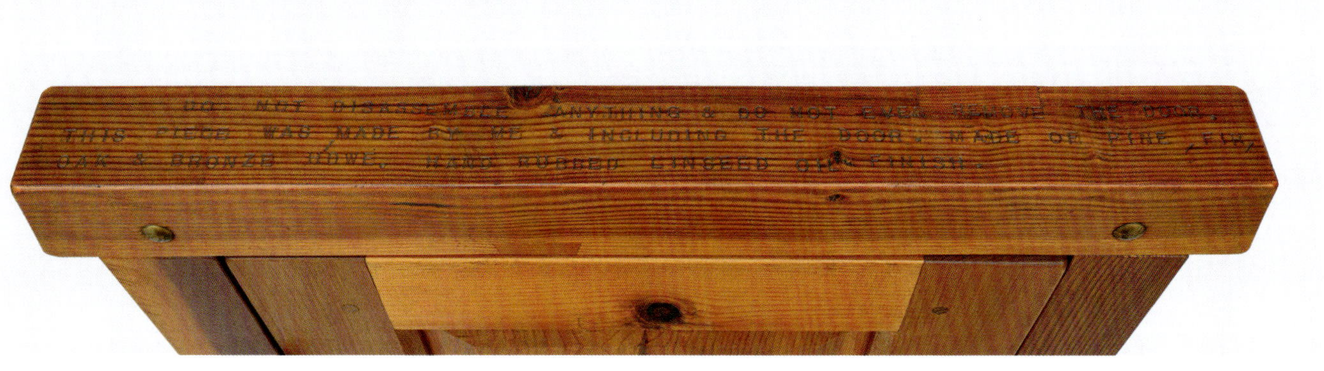
DO NOT DISASSEMBLE ANYTHING & DO NOT EVER REMOVE THE DOOR.
THIS PIECE WAS MADE BY ME & INCLUDING THE DOOR, MADE OF PINE, FIR,
OAK & BRONZE DOWL. HAND RUBBED LINSEED OIL FINISH.

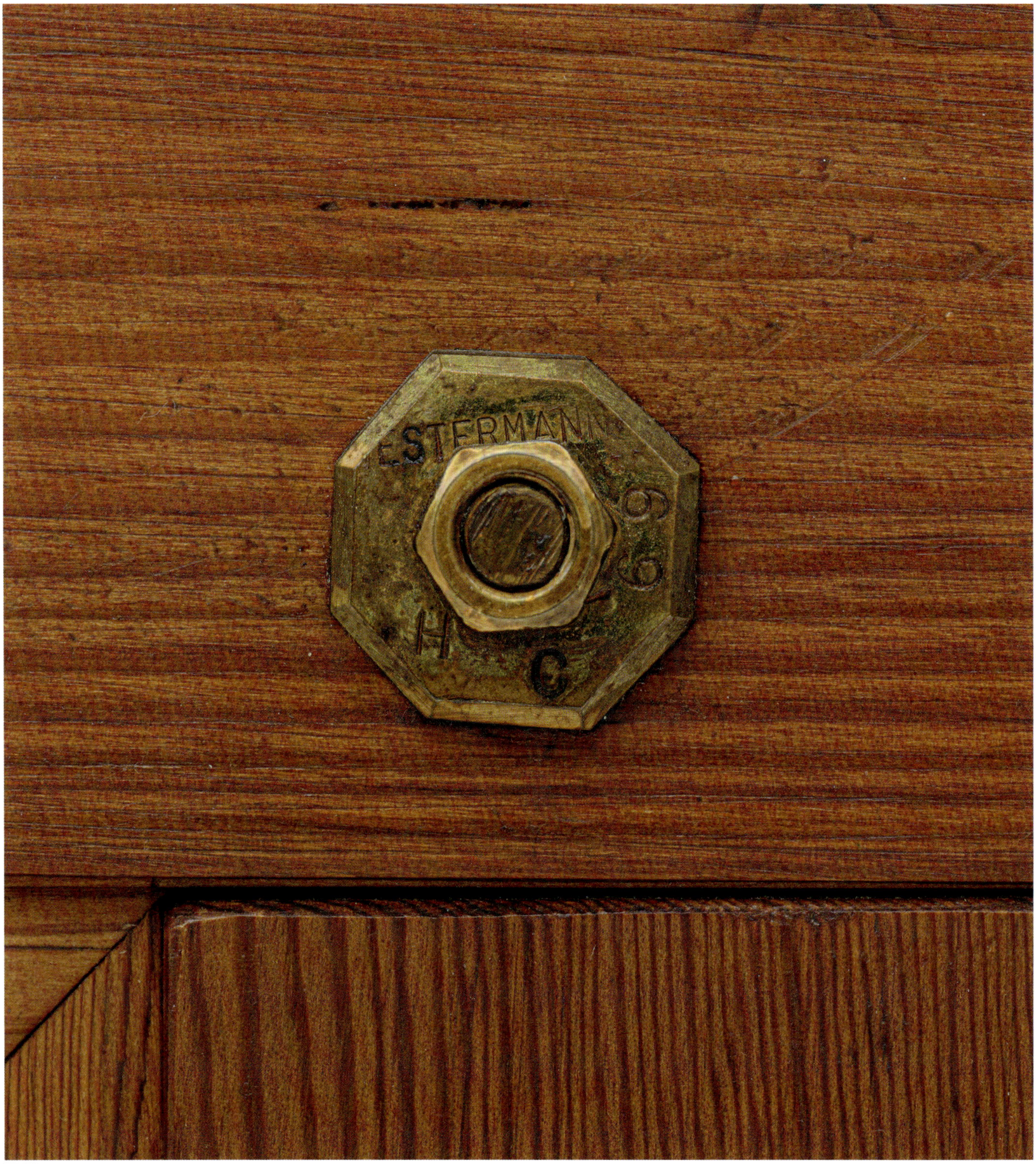

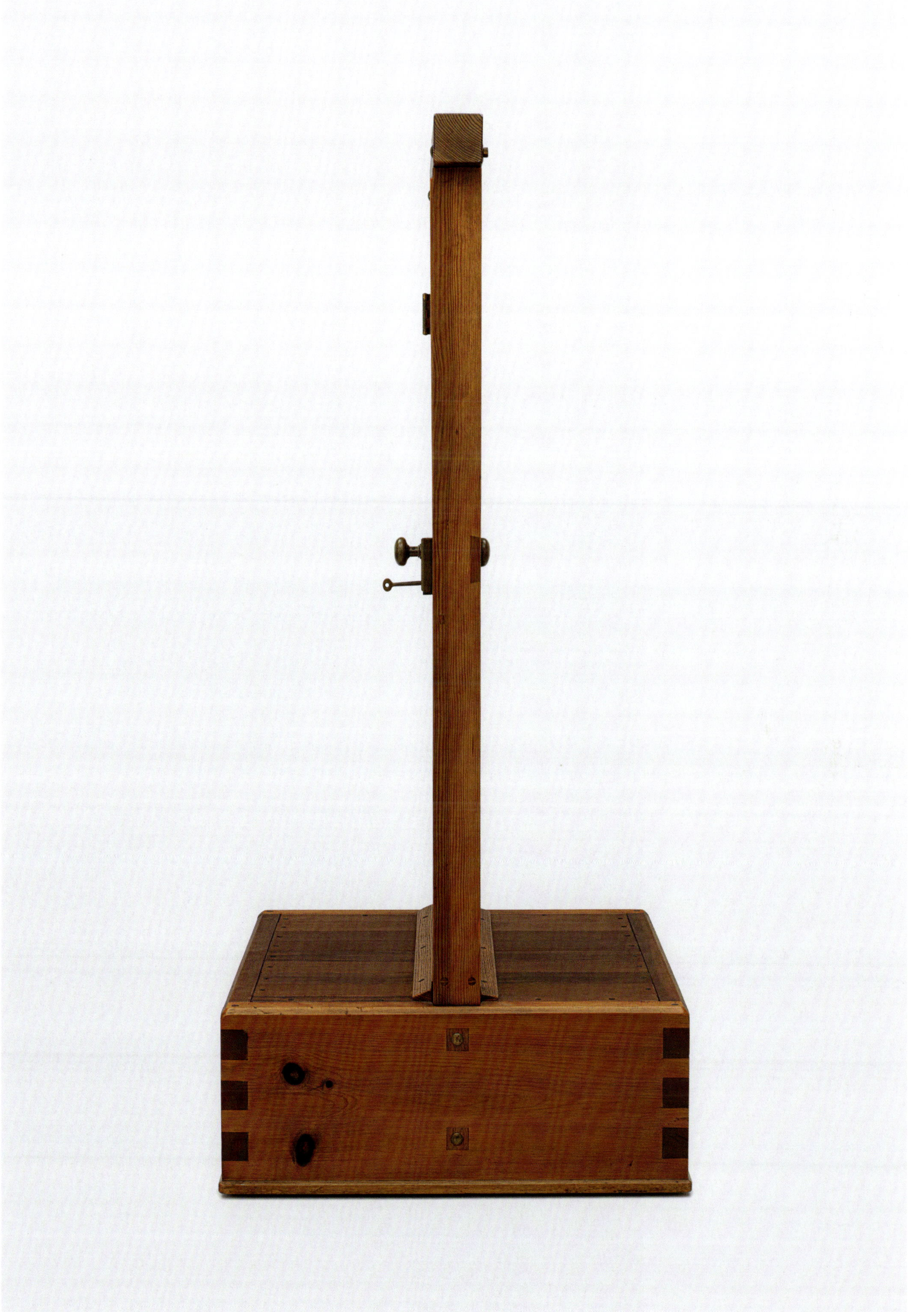

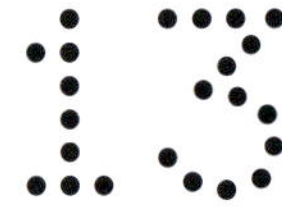

13

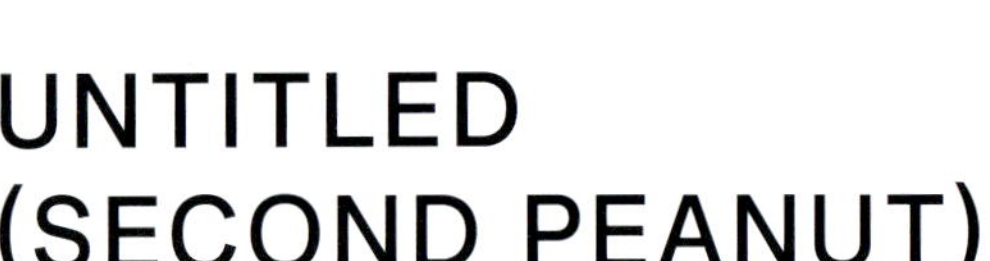

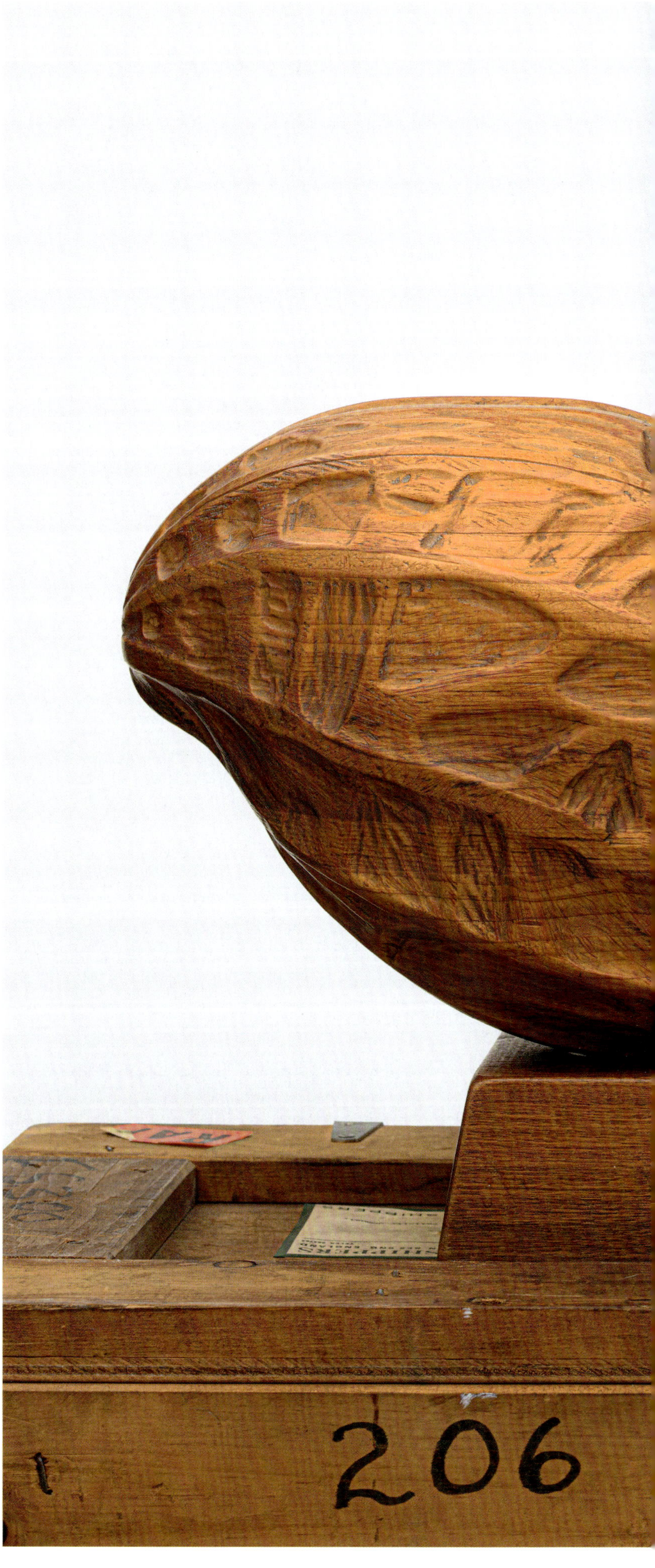

UNTITLED
(SECOND PEANUT)

1973
EASTERN PINE, WALNUT,
AND RUBBER BUMPERS

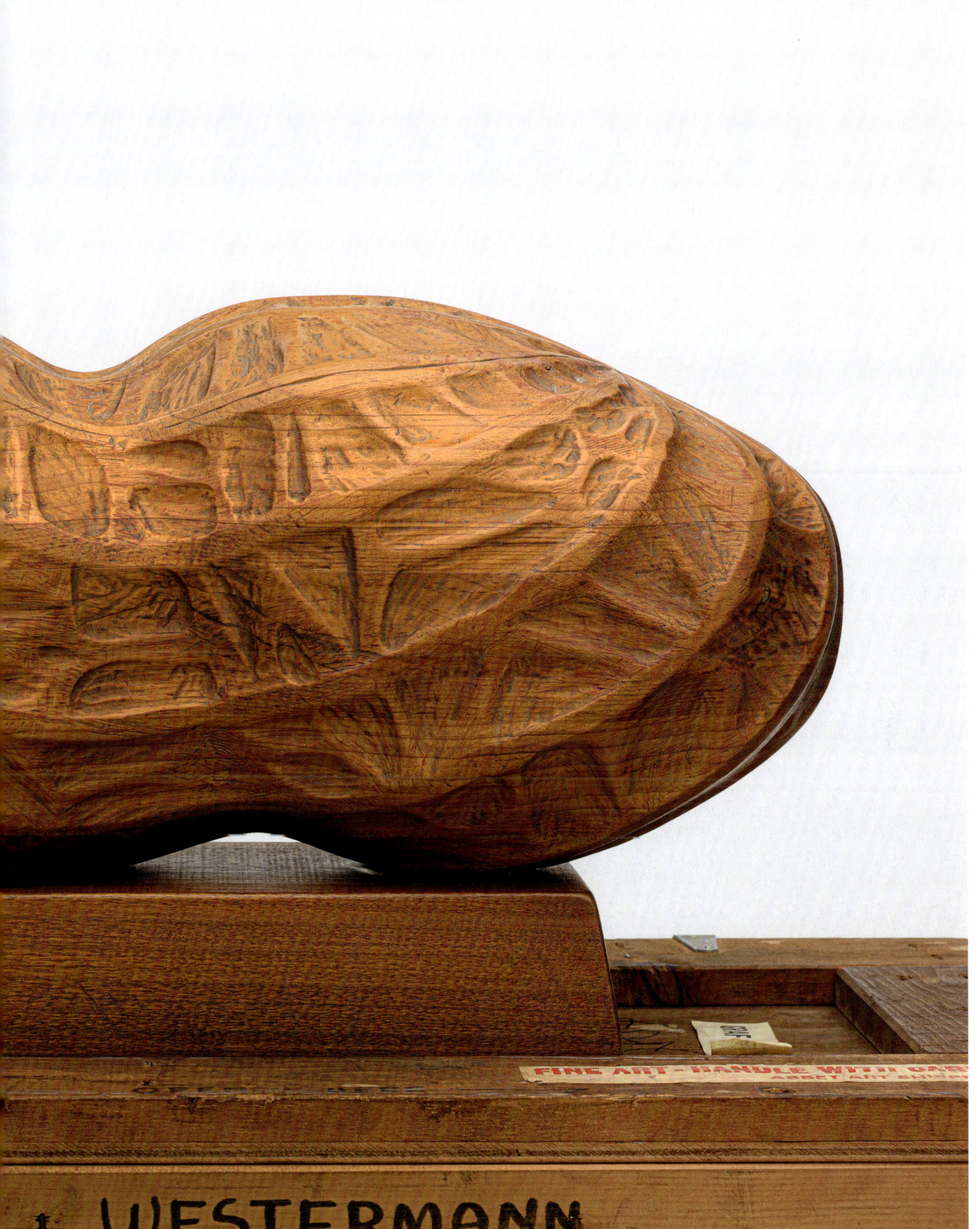

WESTERMANN
FINE ART - HANDLE WITH CARE

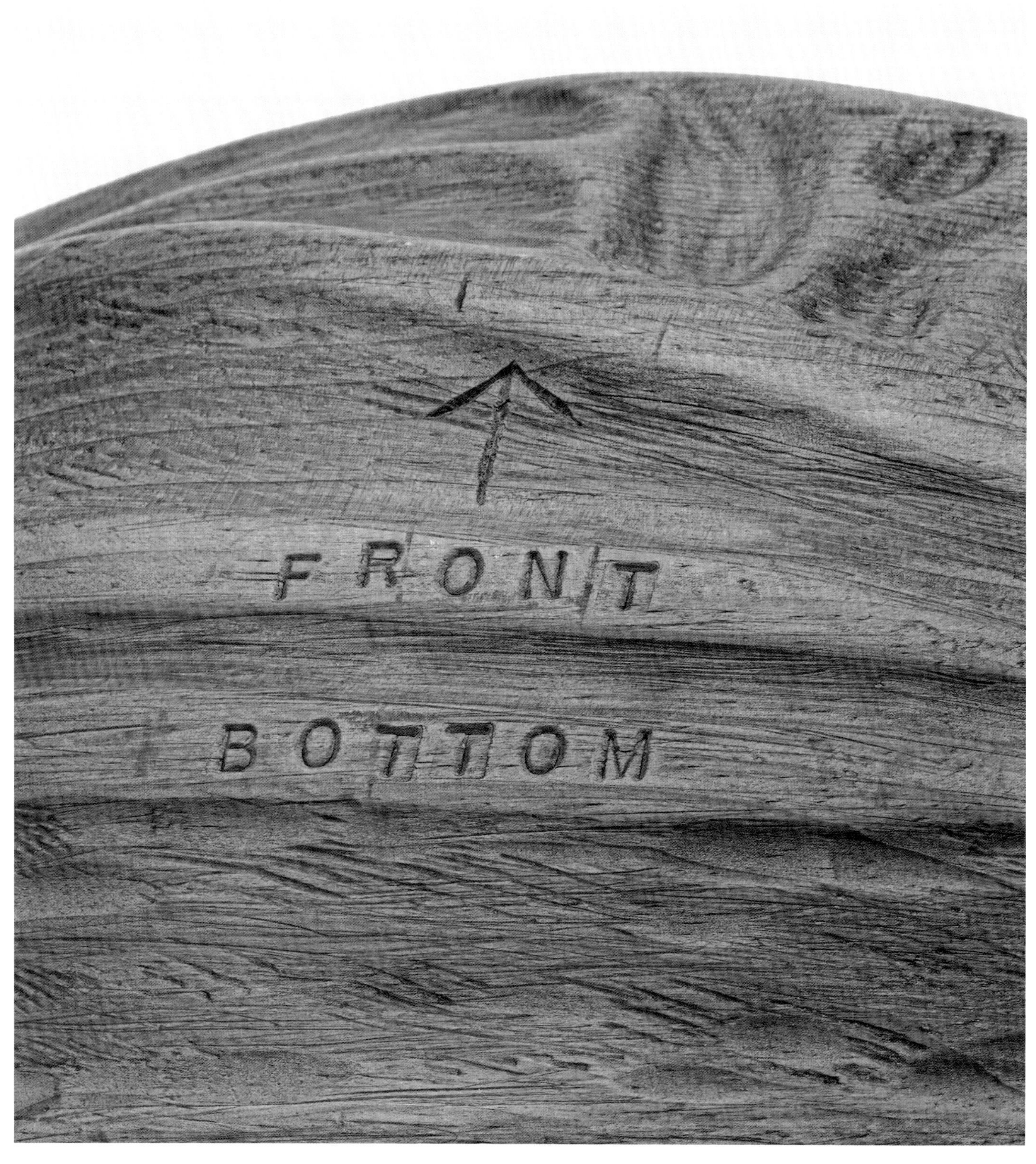

FRONT
BOTTOM

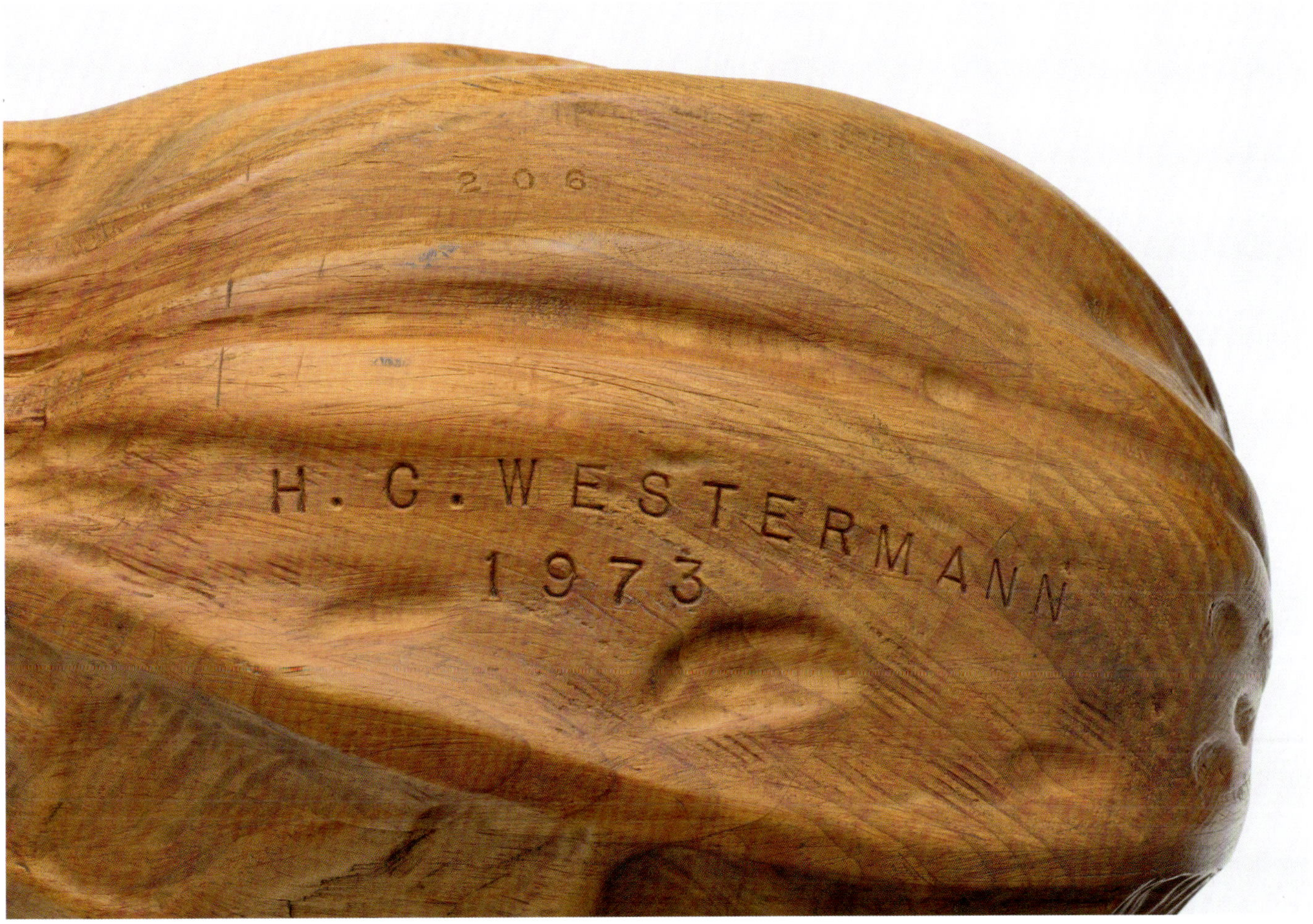

2 0 6
H. C. WESTERMANN
1973

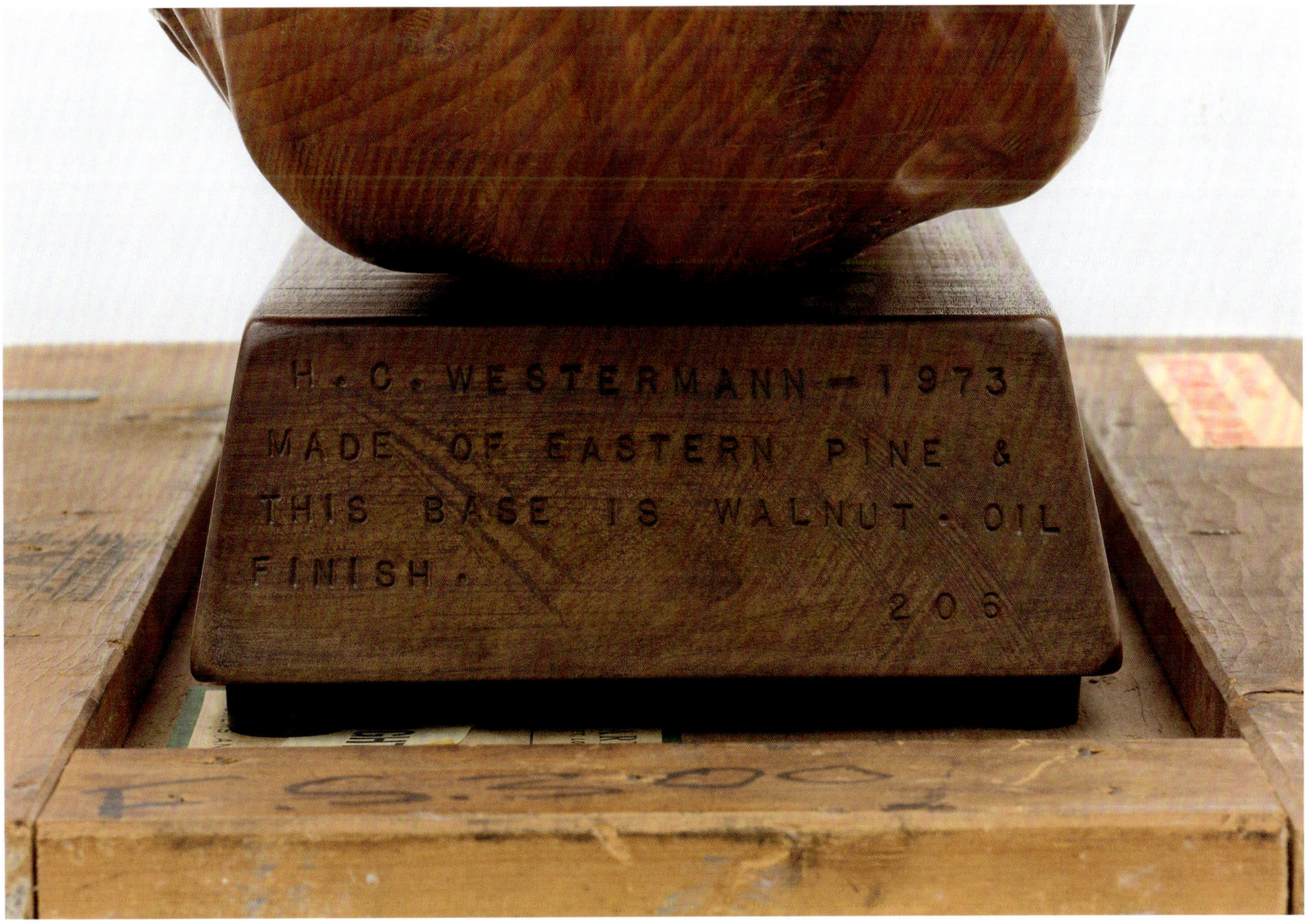

H. C. WESTERMANN — 1973
MADE OF EASTERN PINE. &
THIS BASE IS WALNUT — OIL
FINISH.
2 0 6

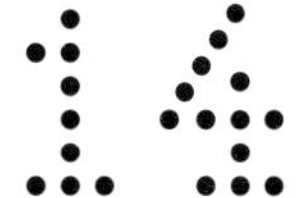

HUTCH THE ONE
ARMED ASTRO-TURF MAN
WITH A DEFENSE

1976
ASTROTURF, PINE, ASPEN, ASH,
CHESTNUT, AND SAPLINGS

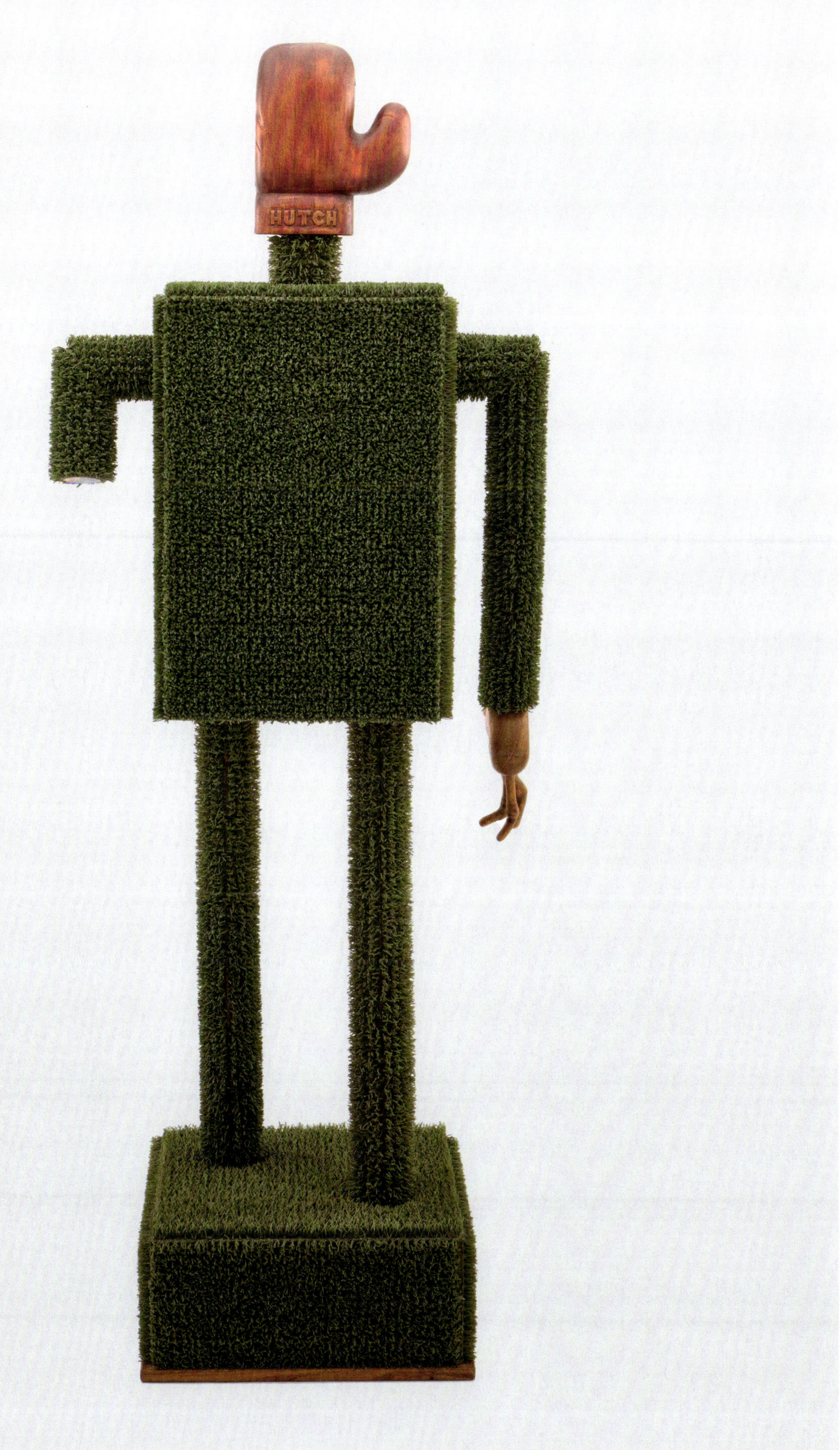
HUTCH

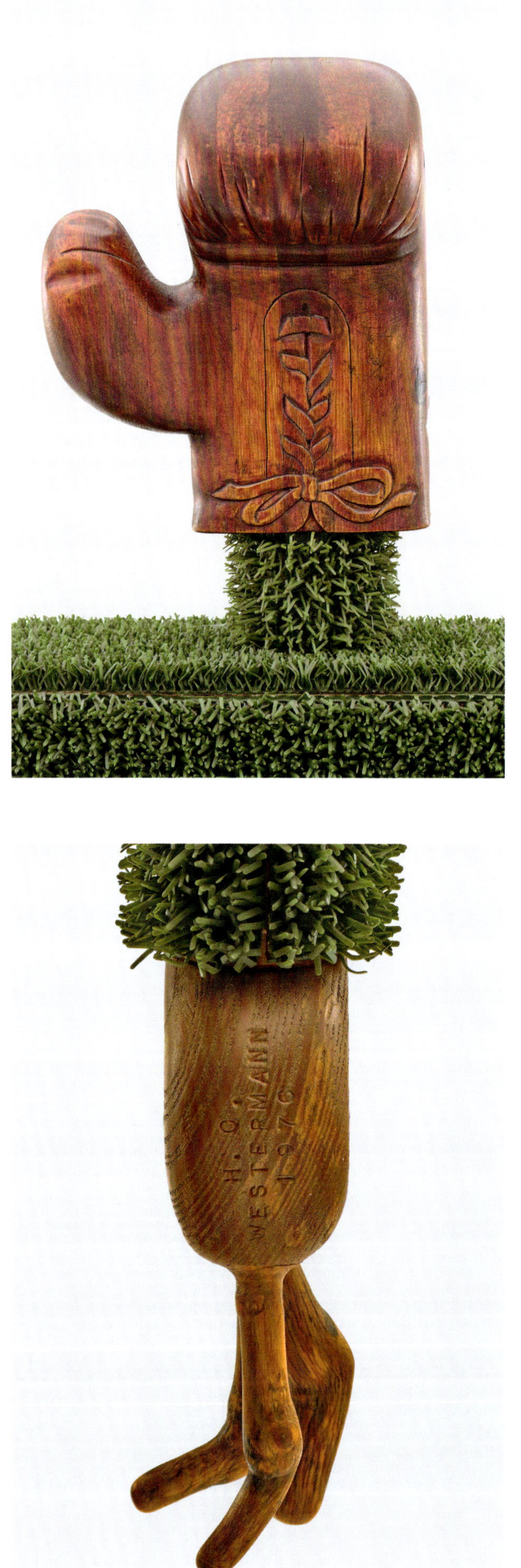
H. C.
WESTERMANN
1976
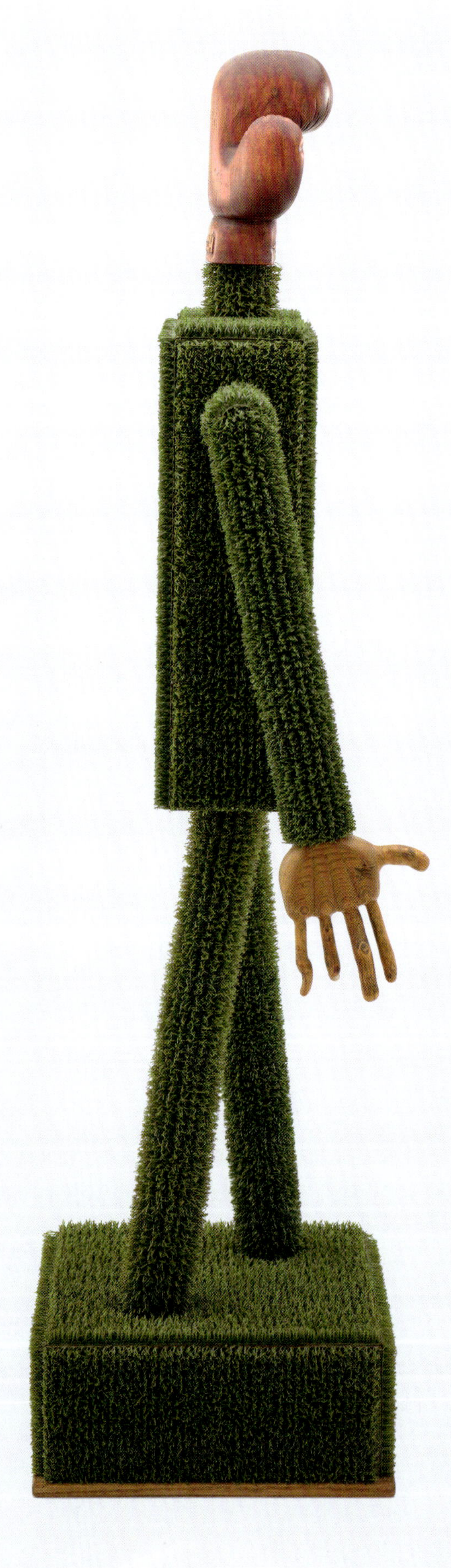

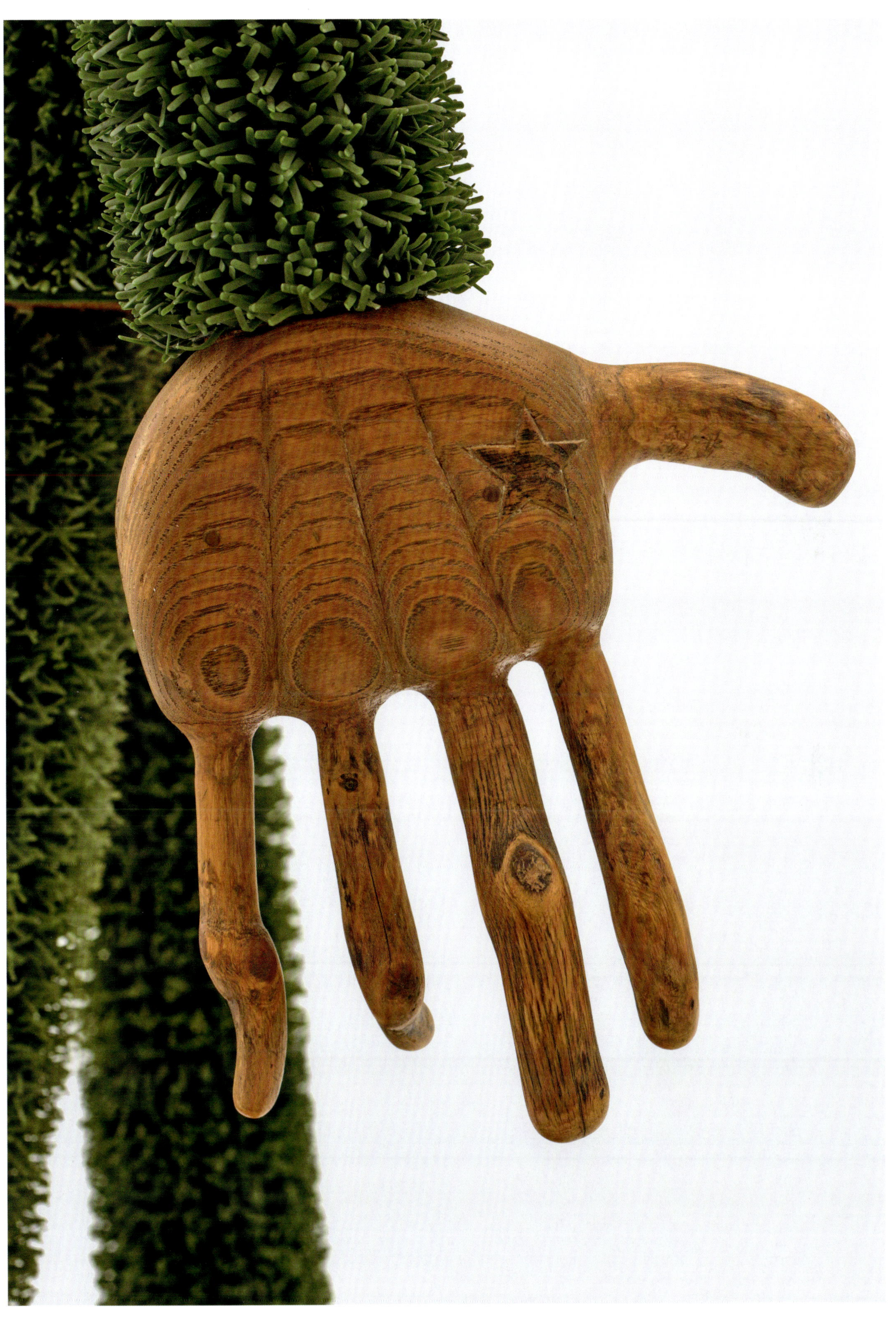

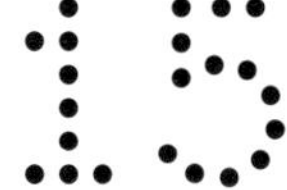

DOVETAILED
HOUSE

1979
PINE, ENAMEL, PLATE GLASS,
LINOLEUM, AND CAST LEAD

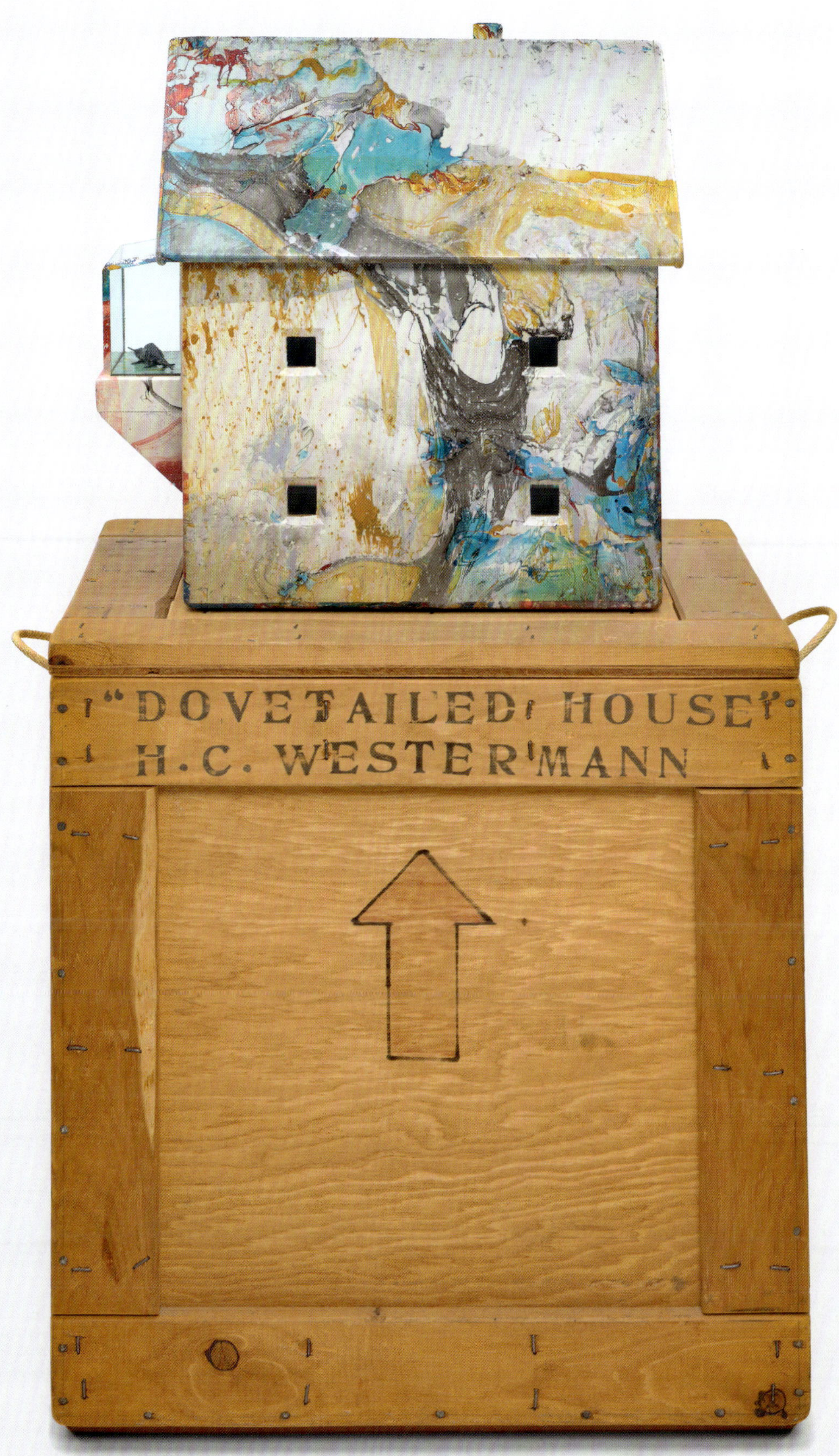

"DOVETAILED HOUSE"
H.C. WESTERMANN

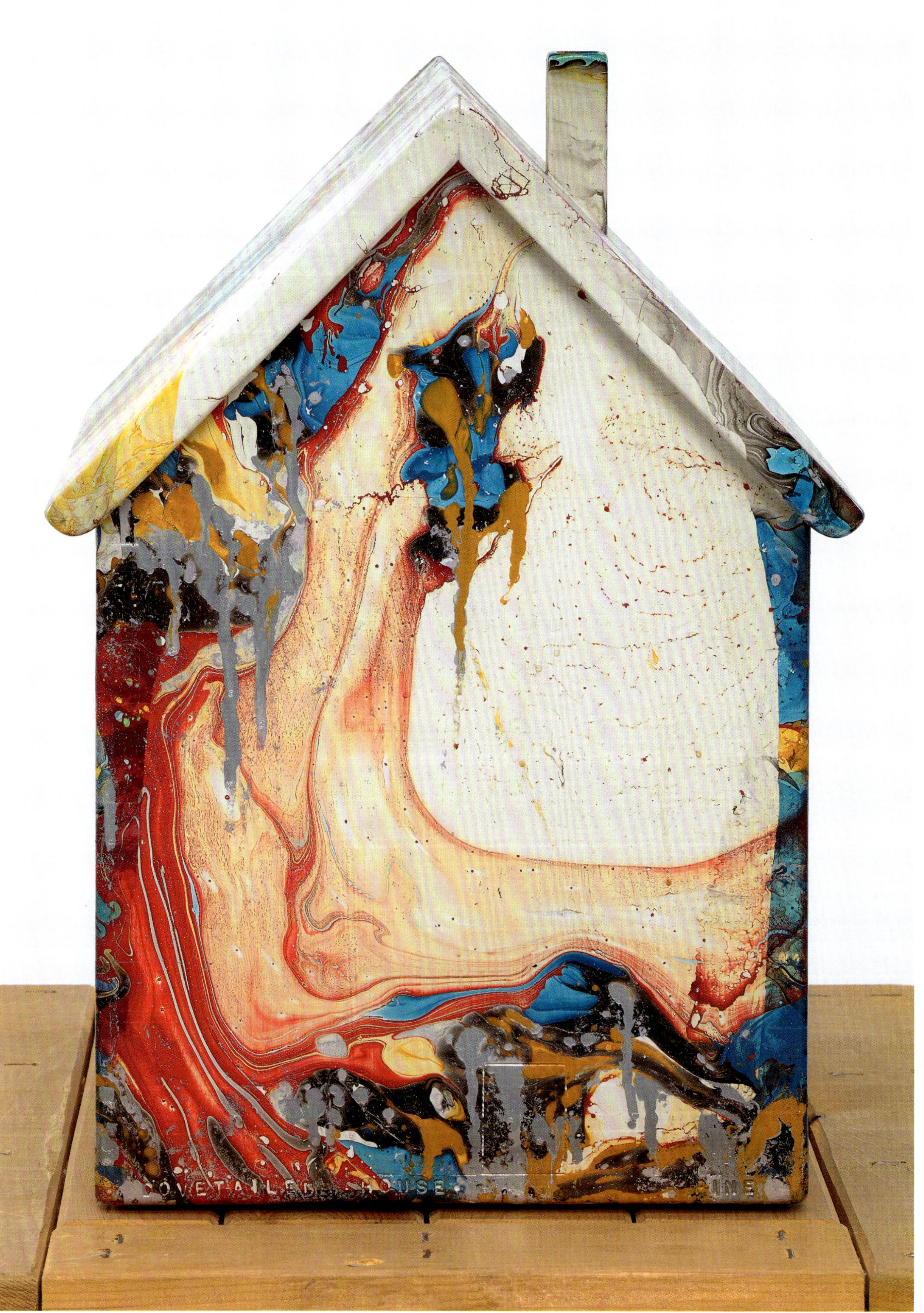
DOVETAILED HOUSE
PINE

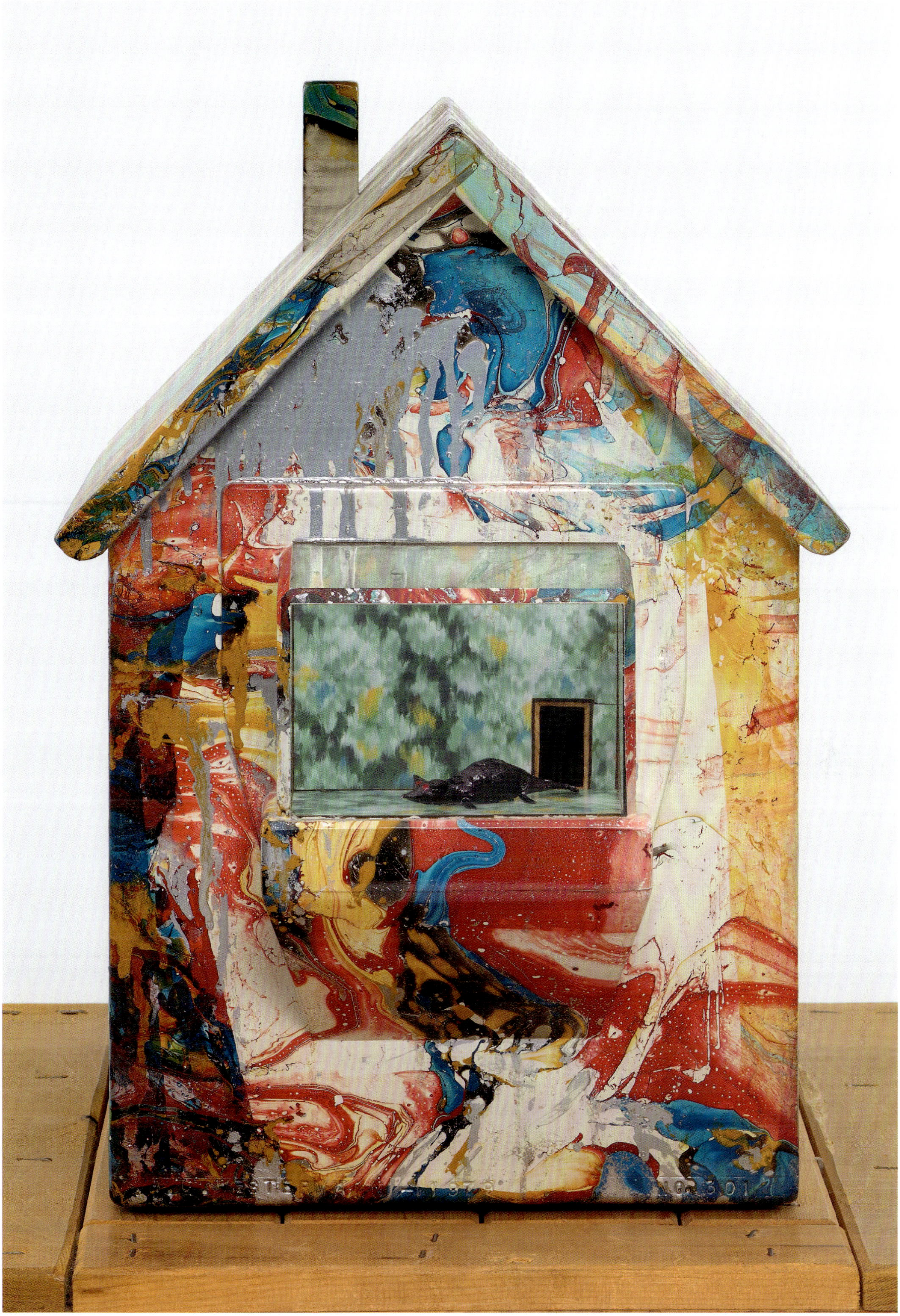

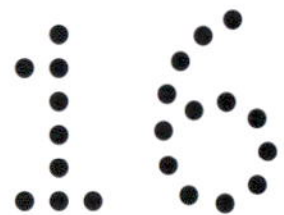

16

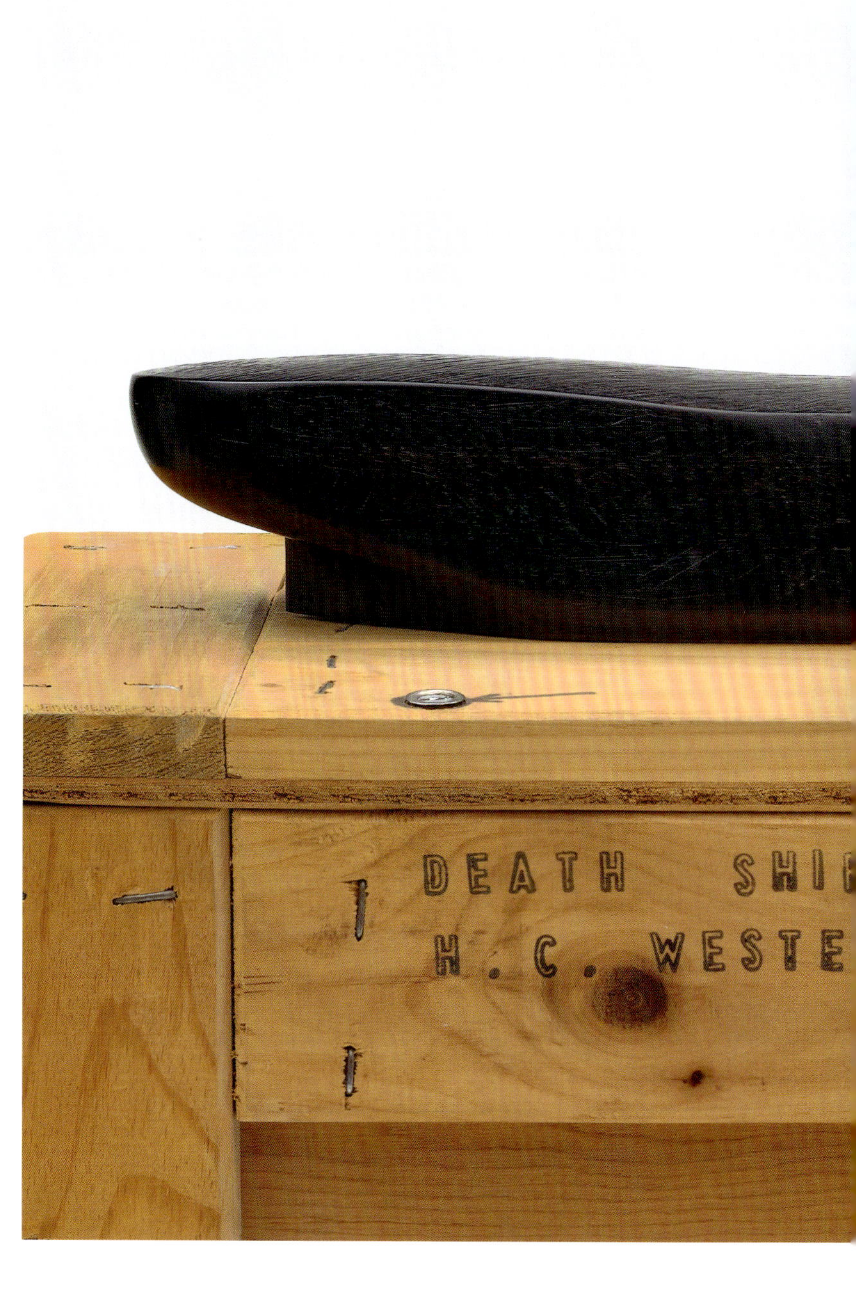

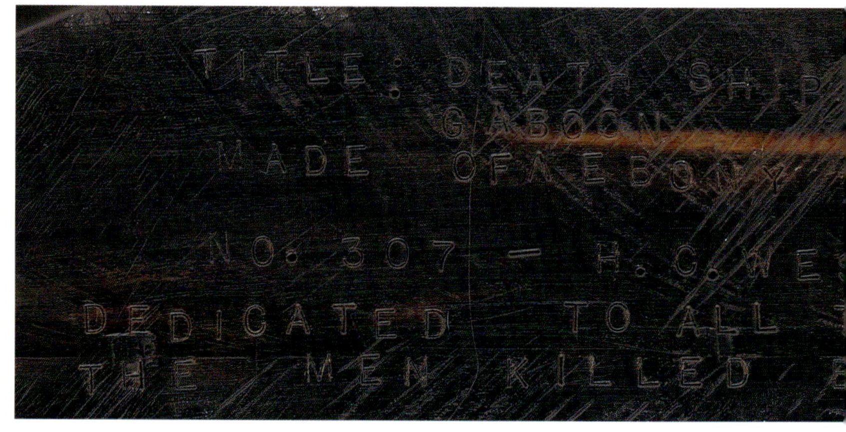

DEATH SHIP,
OUT OF
SAN PEDRO,
ADRIFT

1980
EBONY, BRASS,
AND SOLDER

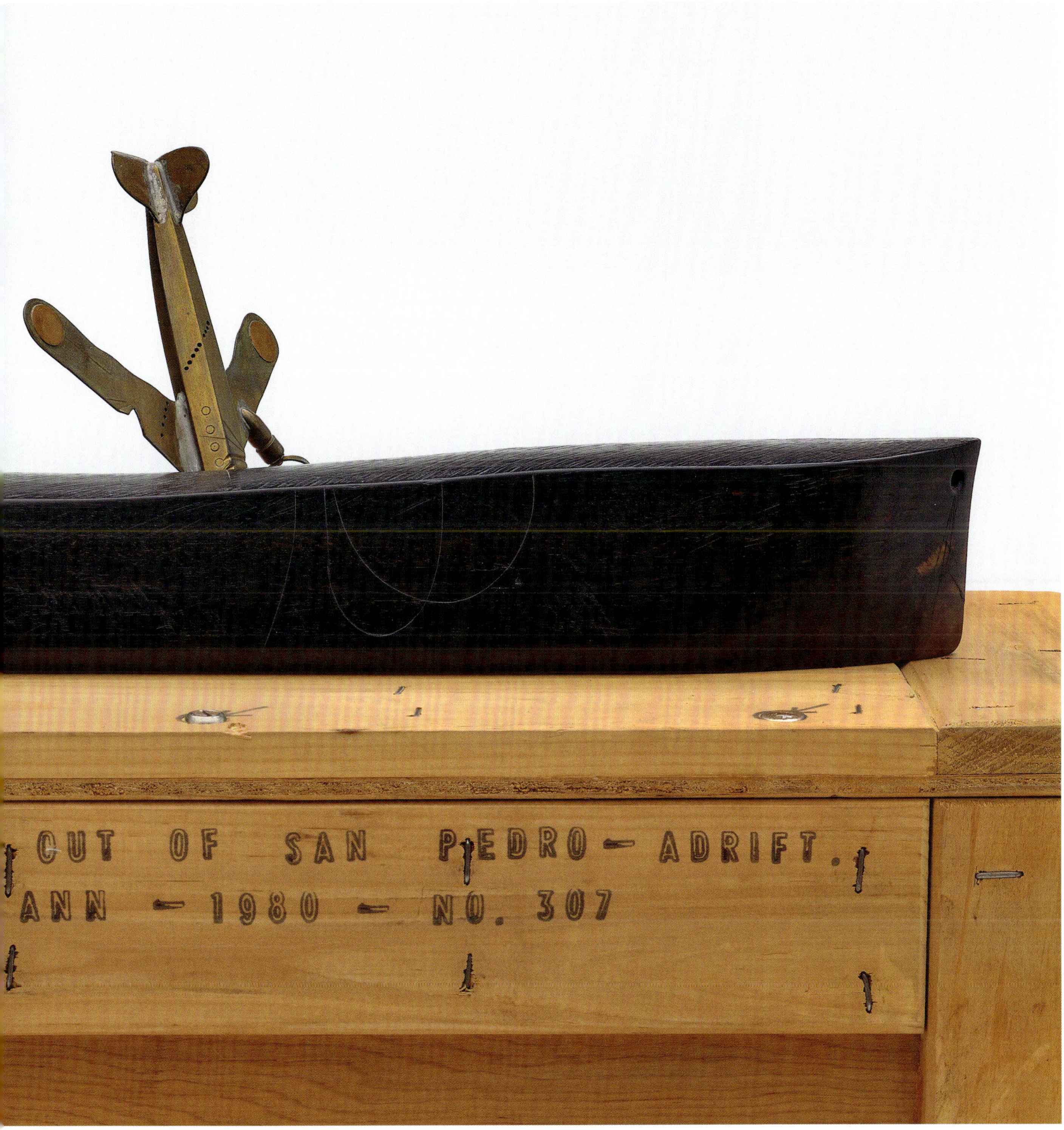

CUT OF SAN PEDRO - ADRIFT.
ANN - 1980 - NO. 307

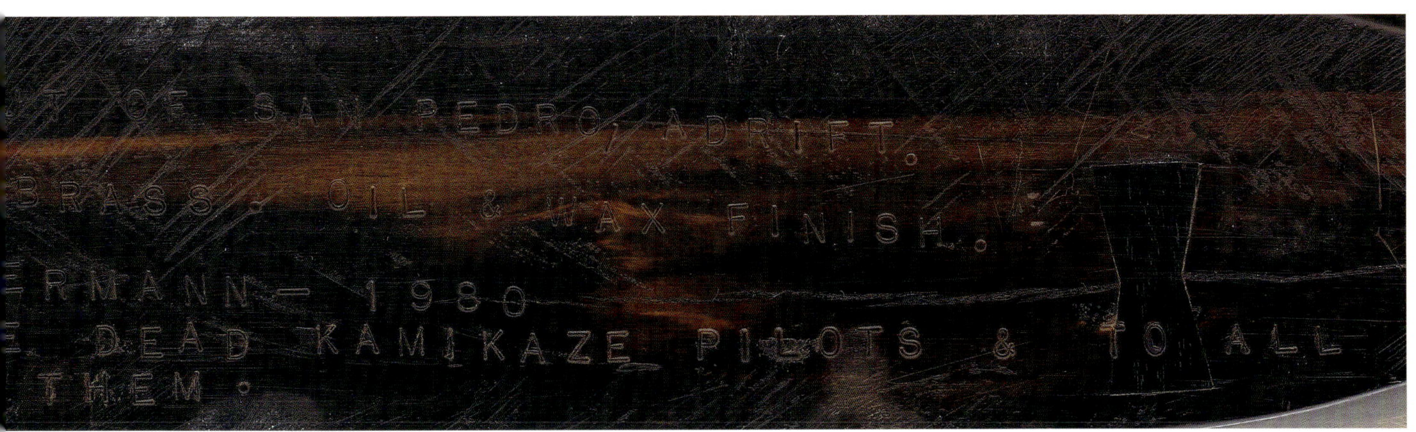
T OF SAN PEDRO - ADRIFT.
BRASS - OIL & WAX FINISH.
RMANN - 1980
DEAD KAMIKAZE PILOTS & TO ALL
THEM.

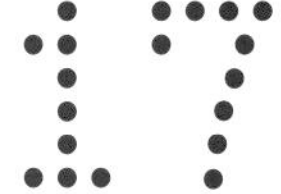

JACK OF DIAMONDS

1981
GALVANIZED WIRE LATH,
GALVANIZED SHEET METAL, GALVANIZED
CORNER BEADING, OAK, PINE,
AND VERMILLION

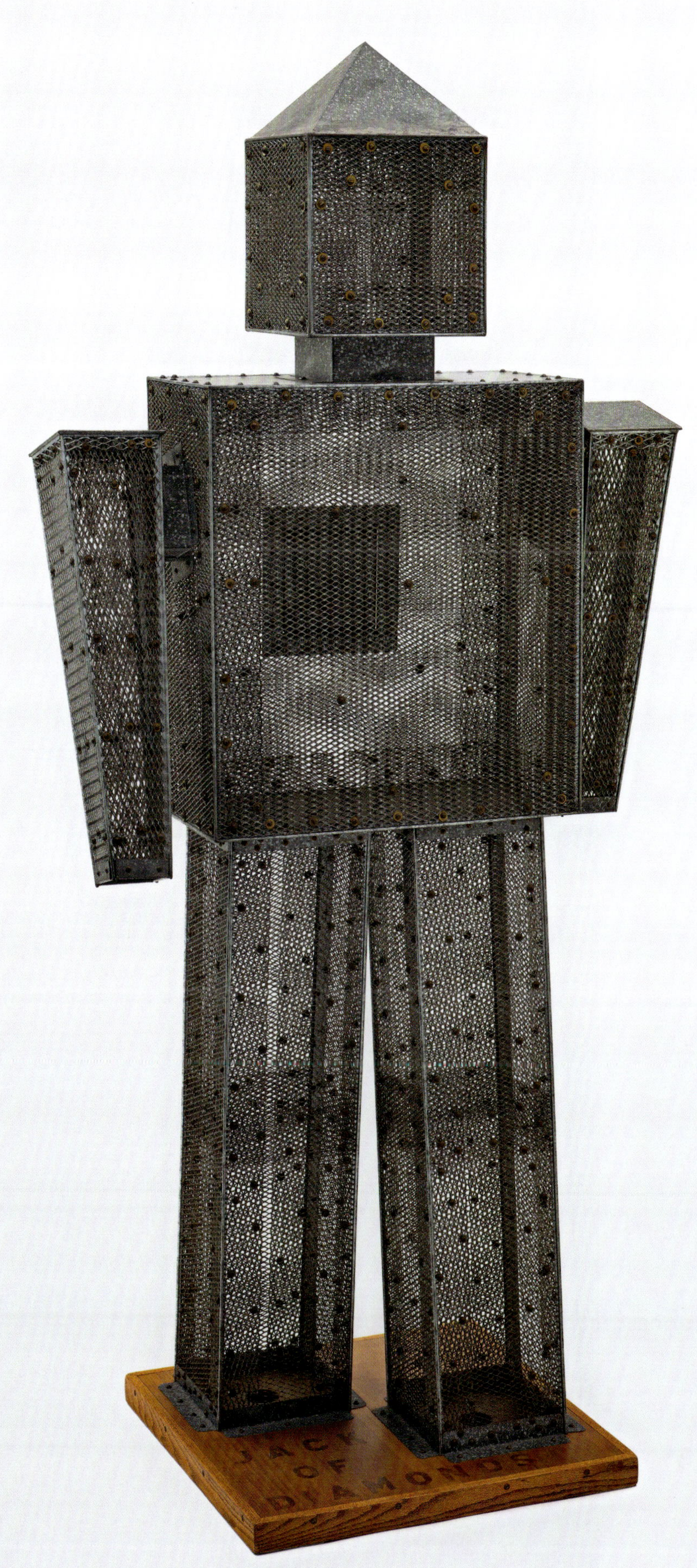

JACK
OF
DIAMONDS

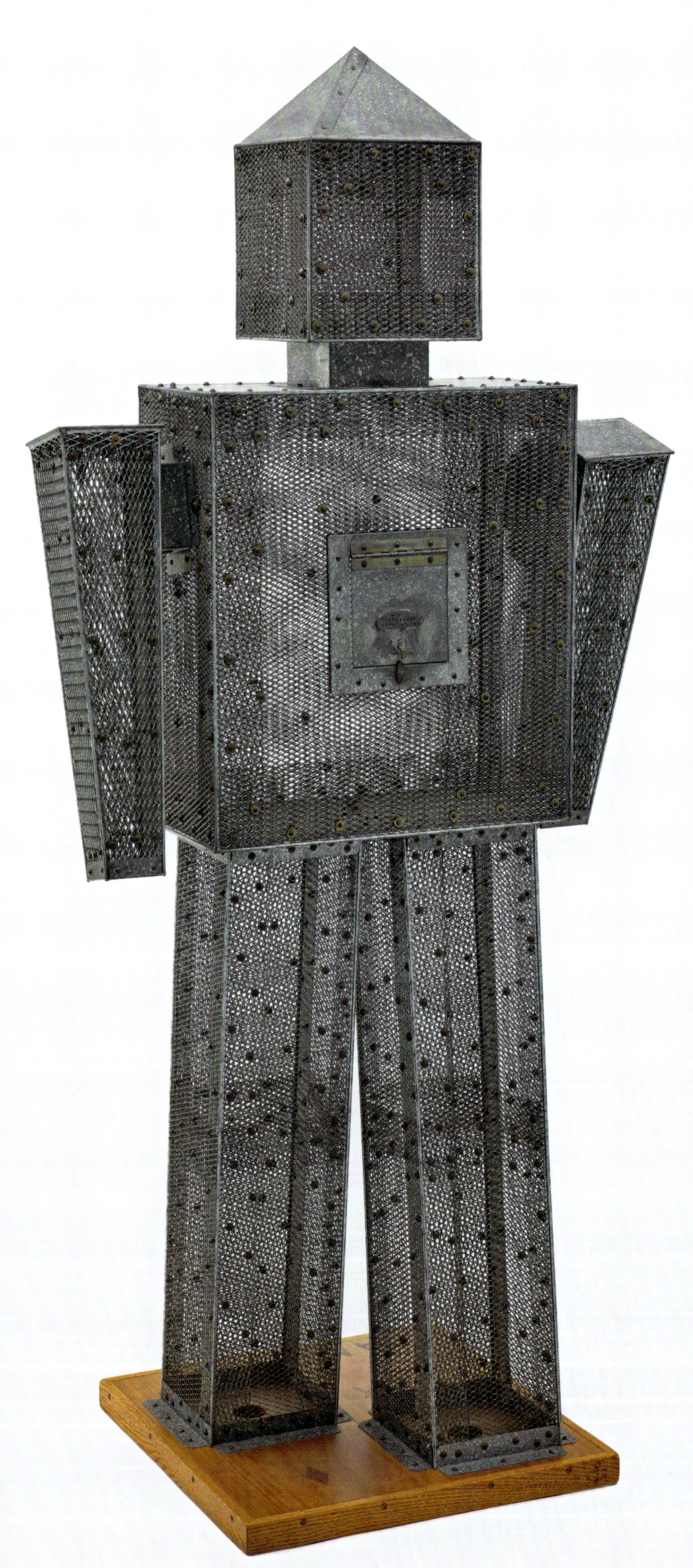

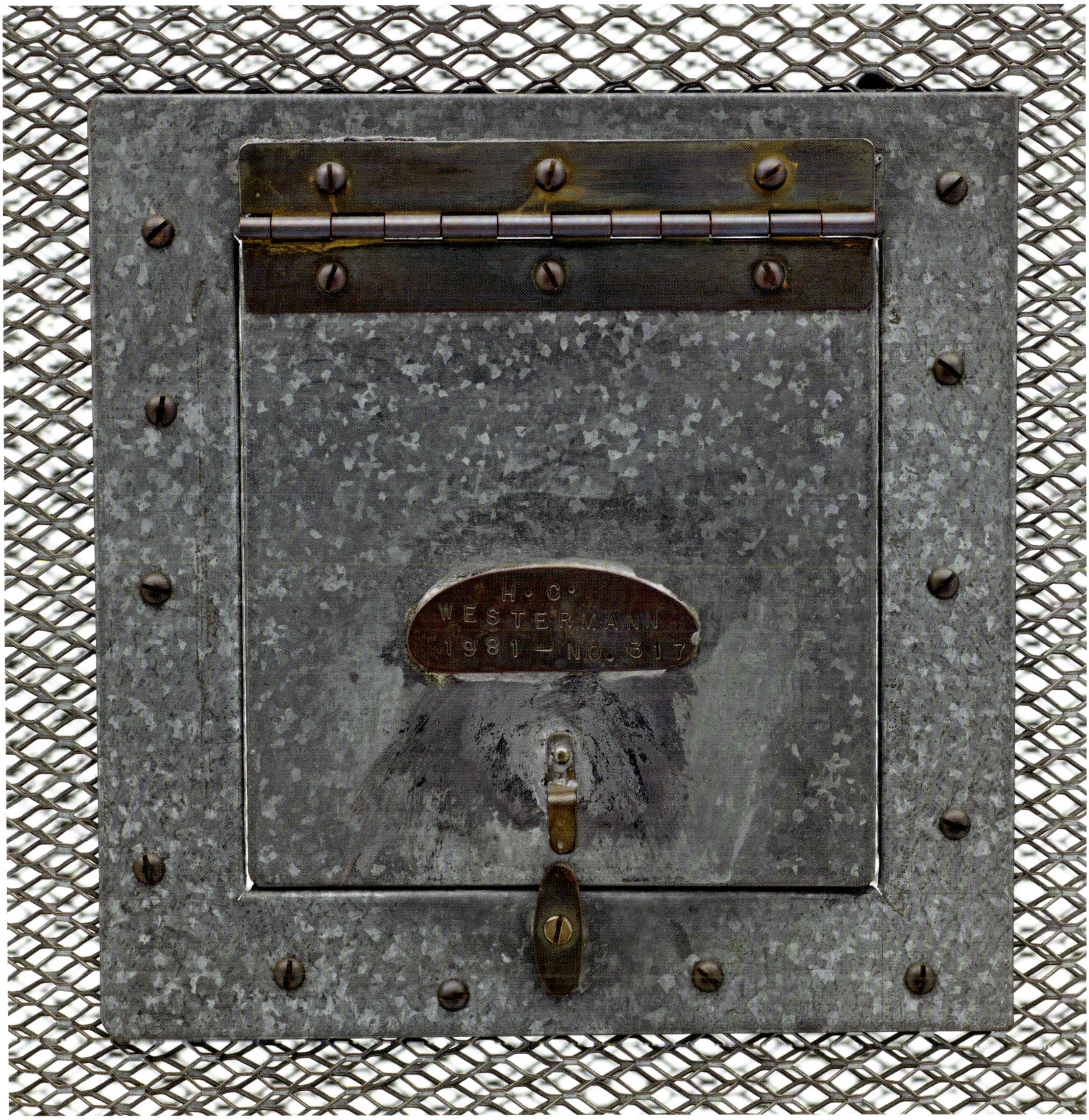

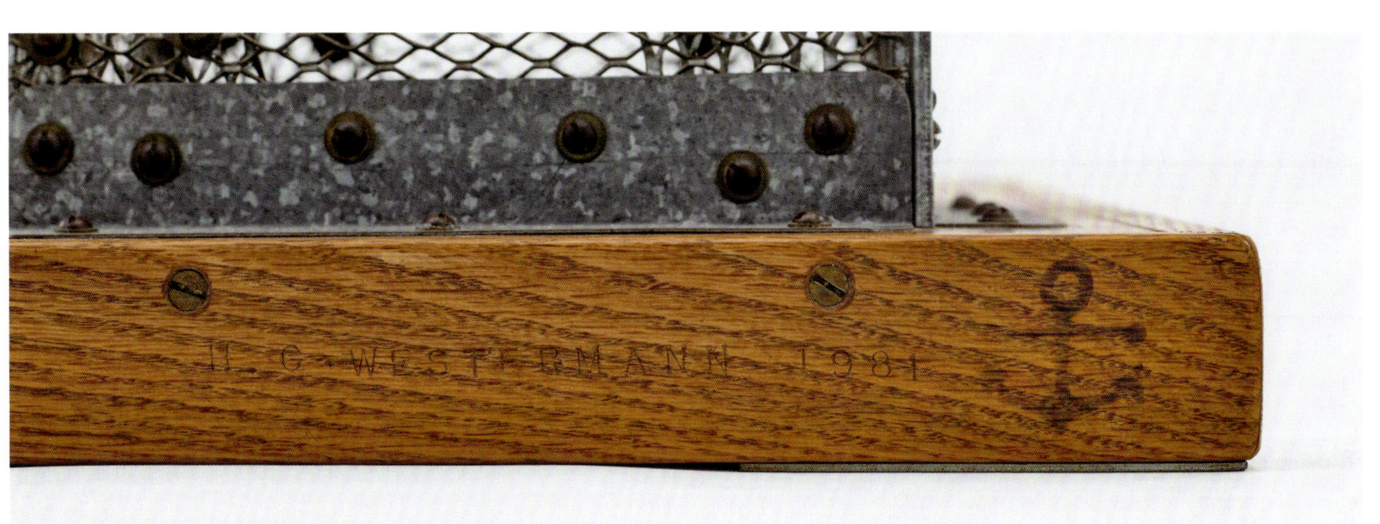

LIST OF WORKS

ALL WORKS ARE BY H. C. (HORACE CLIFFORD) WESTERMANN (AMERICAN, 1922–1981) AND ARE IN THE COLLECTION OF THE ART INSTITUTE OF CHICAGO.

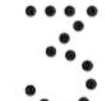 **Uncommitted Little Chicago Child**, 1957
Oak, maple, metal clockface, and paper
decoupage; 75 × 16.9 × 20.4 cm
(29½ × 6⅝ × 8 in.)
Gift of the Estate of Alan and
Dorothy Press in acknowledgment
of their family, 2023.2917

 **Object under Pressure**, 1960
Douglas fir, metal, and pressure gauge;
184.8 × 35.6 × 41.6 cm
(72¾ × 14 × 16⅜ in.)
Gift of the Estate of Alan and
Dorothy Press in acknowledgment
of their family, 2023.2905

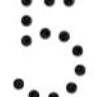 **The Big Change**, 1963
Douglas fir marine plywood, Masonite, and ink;
191.5 × 51.5 × 51.5 cm (75⅜ × 20¼ × 20¼ in.)
Gift of the Estate of Alan and
Dorothy Press in acknowledgment
of their family, 2023.2906

Eclipse #1, 1963
Pine, plate-glass mirror, paint, brass plate,
and rubber bumpers; 25.8 × 25.8 × 14.3 cm
(10⅛ × 10⅛ × 5⅝ in.)
Gift of the Estate of Alan and
Dorothy Press in acknowledgment
of their family, 2023.2916.1–2

The Night Life, 1963
Plate-glass mirror, fir, Masonite, brass plate,
rubber bumpers, and ink; 72.1 × 45.5 × 24.8 cm
(28⅜ × 17⅞ × 9¾ in.)
Gift of the Estate of Alan and
Dorothy Press in acknowledgment
of their family, 2023.2910

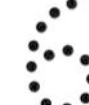 **The Sonic Boom**, 1963
Wood, plate-glass mirror, bubinga, paint, and ink;
55.9 × 45.5 × 13.4 cm (22 × 17⅞ × 5¼ in.)
Gift of the Estate of Alan and
Dorothy Press in acknowledgment
of their family, 2023.2918

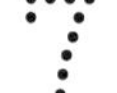 **Homage to American Art
(Dedicated to Elie Nadelman)**, 1966
Douglas fir, ash, cast lead, and antique shovel
handle; 122.6 × 45.8 × 46.4 cm
(48¼ × 18 × 18¼ in.)
Gift of the Estate of Alan and
Dorothy Press in acknowledgment
of their family, 2023.2912

 **Rotting Jet Wing**, 1966
Pine, plate glass, felt, and copper;
98.8 × 69.6 × 37.2 cm (38⅞ × 27⅜ × 14⅝ in.)
Gift of the Estate of Alan and
Dorothy Press in acknowledgment
of their family, 2023.2911

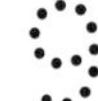 **World's Strongest Glue**, 1966
Solid cast bronze, brass, and paint;
39.7 × 28.3 × 32.1 cm (15⅝ × 11⅛ × 12⅝ in.)
Gift of the Estate of Alan and
Dorothy Press in acknowledgment
of their family, 2023.2919

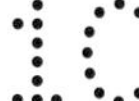 **Control**, 1968
Oak, mahogany, pine, plate glass, tar, chicken
feathers, sheet copper, brass, and solder;
64.8 × 28.9 × 28.9 cm (25½ × 11⅜ × 11⅜ in.)
Gift of the Estate of Alan and
Dorothy Press in acknowledgment
of their family, 2023.2914.1–2

Wet Flower, 1968
Wood, glass, Connecticut fieldstone,
linoleum, dried roots, putty, and varnish;
73.7 × 45.8 × 35.6 cm (29 × 18 × 14 in.)
Gift of the Estate of Alan and
Dorothy Press in acknowledgment
of their family, 2023.2913

Little Egypt, 1969
Douglas fir, pine, oak, and bronze;
174 × 82.3 × 79.1 cm (68½ × 32⅜ × 31⅛ in.)
Gift of the Estate of Alan and
Dorothy Press in acknowledgment
of their family, 2023.2907

Untitled (Second Peanut), 1973
Eastern pine, walnut, and rubber bumpers;
35.6 × 63.5 × 24.2 cm (14 × 25 × 9½ in.)
Gift of the Estate of Alan and
Dorothy Press in acknowledgment
of their family, 2023.2920.1–2

**Hutch the One Armed Astro-Turf
Man with a Defense**, 1976
Astroturf, pine, aspen, ash, chestnut,
and saplings; 190.5 × 73.1 × 54.7 cm
(75 × 28¾ × 21½ in.)
Gift of the Estate of Alan and
Dorothy Press in acknowledgment
of their family, 2023.2908

Dovetailed House, 1979
Pine, enamel, plate glass, linoleum, and cast lead;
48.6 × 35 × 35 cm (19⅛ × 13¾ × 13¾ in.)
Gift of the Estate of Alan and
Dorothy Press in acknowledgment
of their family, 2023.2915.1–2

Death Ship, Out of San Pedro, Adrift, 1980
Ebony, brass, and solder;
17.8 × 60.7 × 16.6 cm (7 × 23⅞ × 6½ in.)
Gift of the Estate of Alan and
Dorothy Press in acknowledgment
of their family, 2023.2904.1–2

Jack of Diamonds, 1981
Galvanized wire lath, galvanized sheet metal,
galvanized corner beading, oak, pine, and
vermillion; 202.6 × 93.4 × 60.1 cm
(79¾ × 36¾ × 23⅝ in.)
Gift of the Estate of Alan and
Dorothy Press in acknowledgment
of their family, 2023.2909

CONTRIBUTORS

GIAMPAOLO BIANCONI is the Dittmer Associate Curator of Modern and Contemporary Art at the Art Institute of Chicago. He was previously a curator at Museum Brandhorst, Munich, where he organized exhibitions including *Site Visit* (2022) and launched the Museum Brandhorst Flag Commission. From 2014 to 2020, he worked at the Museum of Modern Art, New York, where he was a curator for the inaugural reinstallation of MoMA's collection following its 2019 expansion. His writing appears in catalogues including *Dara Birnbaum: Reaction* (Dancing Foxes Press, New York, 2022), *Petra Cortright* (Skira, Milan, 2020), *Agnes Denes: Absolutes and Intermediates* (The Shed, New York, 2019), and *Judson Dance Theater: The Work Is Never Done* (The Museum of Modern Art, New York, 2018), as well as in *Artforum*, *Frieze*, and *Rhizome*.

THEA LIBERTY NICHOLS is Associate Research Curator, Modern and Contemporary Art, at the Art Institute of Chicago. Her prior work for the museum includes co-organizing *Hairy Who? 1966–1969* (2018), with Ann Goldstein and Mark Pascale, and providing support for *Andy Warhol: From A to B and Back Again* (2019) and Ray *Johnson c/o* (2021). Most recently, she co-organized *Christina Ramberg: A Retrospective* (2024) with Pascale.

ED RUSCHA's deadpan representations of Hollywood logos, stylized gas stations, and landscapes distill the imagery of popular culture into a language of cinematic and typographical codes that are as accessible as they are profound. He produced his first artist's book, *Twentysix Gasoline Stations*—a series of deadpan photographs the artist took while driving on Route 66 from Los Angeles to Oklahoma City—in 1963, and represented the United States at the 51st Venice Biennale (2005) with *Course of Empire*, an installation of ten paintings. Working in diverse media, Ruscha continues to influence contemporary artists worldwide with his formal experimentations and clever use of the evolving American vernacular.

INDEX

NOTE: PAGE NUMBERS IN BOLD REFER TO ILLUSTRATIONS.
WORKS BY H. C. WESTERMANN ARE LISTED BY TITLE.
WORKS BY OTHERS ARE FOUND UNDER THE ARTIST'S OR
AUTHOR'S NAME.

Abstract Expressionism, 19, 23, 31
Adorno, Theodor W., 14
Adrian, Dennis, 17, 39
Allan Frumkin Gallery, 29, **29**, 30n3, 32–33, 34.
    See also Frumkin, Allan
Aluminated, **26**
American Sculptors of the Sixties (LACMA,
    1967), 29
Applin, Jo, 16–17
Arneson, Robert, 35, 36
    Head Stand on a Cliff, 35
    "Slant Step," 36
art dealers, 24–25. *See also* Frumkin, Allan
Art Institute of Chicago, 18, 31, 34
Art of Assemblage (MoMA, 1961), 15, 16

Bay Area Figuration, 30
Beall, Joanna (married to Westermann),
    23, 29, 34
Beall, Lester, 23
Bell, Larry, 21
Bengston, Billy Al, 21, **21**, 24, **28**, 34–35
Berlant, Tony, 21
The Big Change (pl. 3), **10**, 17, **51–55**
boxes, handcrafted, 27, 39
Brando, Marlon, 11, **11**
Brookfield, CT, 23, 29
Buchloh, Benjamin, 18
Butterfly, 29

Campoli, Cosmo, 31
Canby, Vincent, 11
Canright, Sarah, 30n7, 32, 37, **38**
Carlson, Cynthia, 32
Chicago Imagist Art (MCA, 1972), 29n2, **31**, 32
Chicago Imagists, 16, 19, 29, 29n2, 32
Collins, Jess, **18**
Conceptual Art, 16, 29n2
Conner, Bruce, 15, **18**
Control (pl. 10), **75–79**
Cornell, Joseph, 15, 18

Dada, 27, 29n2
Dada, Surrealism, and Their Heritage (MoMA, 1968), 16
De Forest, Roy, 36
Death Ship, Out of San Pedro, Adrift (pl. 16), 14,
    100–101
death ship motif, 14
Dilexi Gallery, Los Angeles and San Francisco, 29, 34
The Disappearance (boat), **12**
Documenta 5 (Kassel, Germany, 1972), 18–19
Dovetailed House (pl. 15), **97–99**
Dust Pan (for Joanna), 23–24, **24**

Eclipse #1 (pl. 4), **57–59**
The Evil New War God (S.O.B.), 29
Exhibition Momentum counter-salon (1956 and
    1957), 31

Famous Artists from Chicago (Sacramento State
    College, 1970), 30n3
Finish Fetish, 35
Fleming, Ian, 14
Flood, Ed, 30n7, 32, 33, 37, **38**
    Zulu Too Flaming Comet, 33, **33**
folk art, 23
Frumkin, Allan, 17, 18, 19, 24–25, 29. *See also*
    Allan Frumkin Gallery
functional art, 23–24, 25, **24**, 27
Funk Art, 16, 29

Gardner, Leonard, 27
    Fat City (book), 27

gifts, handcrafted, 24, **24**, 25, 27, 37–39
Golub, Leon, 31–32
    Gigantomachy, **31**
Green, Art, 32, 33–34
    Examine the Facts, Consider the Options,
    Apply the Logic, 34, **34**

Haacke, Hans, 18
Hairy Who? (SFAI, 1968), 30n3

Halstead, Whitney, 32
The Hands, 33n12
H. C. Westermann (Frumkin Gallery, 1961), **29**
Heartfield, John, 14–15, 27
    Untitled (Diagnosis), **15**
He-Whore, 32
Homage to American Art (Dedicated to Elie Nadelman) (pl. 7), **67–69**
Human Concern/Personal Torment (University of California, Berkeley, 1970), 29n2
Hutch the One Armed Astro-Turf Man with a Defense (pl. 14), **93–95**

Imagism. *See* Chicago Imagists
influence on other artists, 17, 30, 33–35
interiors, inaccessible or empty, 12, 19. *See also* secret compartments

Jack of Diamonds (pl. 17), **103–5**
Johnson, Ray, 37
Judd, Donald, 15, 16, 17

King, David, 30
Korean War, 12, 17, 30, 35
Kozloff, Max, 37
Kuh, Katharine, 29
Kuspit, Donald, 12

Le Bandeur, 39
Le Kequee (After Jockomedy), 36
Leaf, June, 31
letters, illustrated, **22**, 23, 30n7, 33, 37, **38**
linguistic play, 21, 35–36
Little Egypt (pl. 12), 16n13, 18–19, **19**, **85–87**
Los Angeles, 21, 25, 29, 30
Los Angeles County Museum of Art (LACMA), 29
Lozingot, Serge, 39

Machine for Calculating Risks, 33n12
Made in Chicago (MCA, 1975), 29
Magritte, René, 37n20

mail art movement, 37
Male, American, 32
Memorial to the Idea of Man If He Was an Idea, 39
methods and materials, 15, 23, 25, 33, 33n12, 36
Mies van der Rohe, Ludwig, 29
Minimalism, 16, 29n2
Monster Roster, 30, 31–32
Moore, Henry, 16–17
Moses, Ed, 21, **28**
Museum of Contemporary Art Chicago (MCA), 29, 29n2, **31**, 32
Museum of Modern Art (MoMA), 15, 31
The Mysteriously Abandoned New Home, 12, **13**, **18**, 34

Nauman, Bruce, 16–18, 34–35, 36
    Henry Moore Bound to Fail (Back View), 16–17
    Knot Becoming an Ear (Knot Hearing Well), 17, **17**
    "Slant Step," 36
    Square Knot (H. C. Westermann), 35
    Walking in an Exaggerated Manner around the Perimeter of a Square, 35
    Westermann's Ear, **16**, 16–17, 35
Nelson, Rolf, 24–25
Neo-Dada, 16
New Images of Man (MoMA, 1959), 16, 31
New Left, 30
The Night Life (pl. 5), 33, **61–63**
Nilsson, Gladys, 19, 30n3, 32
Nitsch, Hermann, 18
Nothing Is to Be Done for William T. Wiley, 39
Nutt, Jim, 19, 30n3, 32–33
    Miss E. Knows, 33
    Wowidow, 33

Object under Pressure (pl. 2), 32, **47–49**

Palermo, Blinky, 18
Penn, Arthur
    The Missouri Breaks (film), 11, **11**
Petlin, Irving, 33n8
Polke, Sigmar, 18

Pop Art, 16
Press, Alan, 6, 25
Press, Dorothy, 6, 25
Price, Happy, 34n9, 35–36
Price, Ken, 21, **28**, 34n9, 34–35
Pynchon, Thomas, 14

Rauschenberg, Robert, 15
Renaissance Society, University of Chicago, 29n2
Richter, Gerhard, 18
Rotting Jet Wing (pl. 8), 15, **71**
Rubin, William S., 16
Ruscha, Ed, 11, 15, 18, 21–27, 34–35
    Bloated Empire, Stuffed Regime, 35, **35**

Samaras, Lucas, 18
San Francisco, 29, 34
San Francisco Art Institute (SFAI), 34
San Francisco Museum of Modern Art, 30n3
São Paulo Biennial, 12th (1973), 18–19, 18n17
Saul, Peter, 16, 36
School of the Art Institute of Chicago (SAIC),
    30, 31, 33
secret compartments, 25. *See also* interiors,
    inaccessible or empty
See America First, 21, **36**, 37
Seitz, William C., 15
Selz, Peter, 16
shadow boxes, 15, 33
shipping crates, custom, 27, 33
The Sonic Boom (pl. 6), **65**
Spero, Nancy, 31
Speyer, A. James, 18
Surplus Slop from the Windy City (SFAI, 1970), 30n3
Surrealism, 30, 30n3
Szeemann, Harald, 18

Tamarind Lithography Workshop, 34–37

Uncommitted Little Chicago Child (pl. 1), **43–45**
Untitled (for Happy Price), 39

Untitled (McGovern Pin–Log Cabin), **27**
Untitled (Second Peanut) (pl. 13), **88–91**
USS *Enterprise* ("Galloping Ghost"), 12, 14, 21

war, 12, 14, 21, 30
Westermann, H. C., **10**, **12**, **20**, **21**, **28**, **29**
    about, 11–12
    Americanness of, 17
    athleticism and handstands, **21**, 21, **22**, 23,
        31–32, 35
    cartoon personas, 21, 31
    handyman side job, 33
    humor, sense of, 36
    influence on other artists, 17, 30, 33–35
    letters, illustrated, **22**, 23, 30n7, 33, 37, **38**
    masculinity, 11, 32
    military experiences, 12, 14, 21, 30
    politics of, 27, 30, 35
    self-portraiture, 30n7, 36
    studio, 23, 25
    teaching, 34
    tools, 23

Wet Flower (pl. 11), 33n12, **81–83**
Wiley, William T., 16, 18, 34, 36, 39
    "Slant Step," 36
Wirsum, Karl, 30n3
wordplay, 15, 21, 35–36
World War II, 12, 14, 21
World's Strongest Glue (pl. 9), **73**

H. C. WESTERMANN: ANCHOR CLANKER WAS PUBLISHED
IN CONJUNCTION WITH AN EXHIBITION OF THE SAME
TITLE ORGANIZED BY THE ART INSTITUTE OF CHICAGO,
ON VIEW FROM MAY 17, 2025, TO MAY 17, 2026.

FIRST EDITION
PRINTED IN ITALY

ISBN: 978-0-300-28201-6 (HARDCOVER)

LIBRARY OF CONGRESS CONTROL NUMBER: 2024952010

PUBLISHED BY
THE ART INSTITUTE OF CHICAGO
111 SOUTH MICHIGAN AVENUE
CHICAGO, IL 60603-6404
ARTIC.EDU

DISTRIBUTED BY
YALE UNIVERSITY PRESS
302 TEMPLE STREET
P. O. BOX 209040
NEW HAVEN, CT 06520-9040
YALEBOOKS.COM/ART

EDITED BY SHEILA MAJUMDAR
PRODUCTION BY BEN BERTIN AND LAUREN MAKHOLM
PHOTOGRAPHY RESEARCH BY JOSEPHINE YANASAK-LESZCZYNSKI
PROOFREADING BY DAVID B. OLSEN
INDEXING BY SCOTT SMILEY
PHOTOGRAPHY BY NATHAN KEAY, ROBERT LIFSON, JONATHAN
MATHIAS, JUAN MOLINA HERNÁNDEZ, AND JOE TALLARICO
POSTPRODUCTION BY KAITLYN FULTZ-CAMPION
PREPRODUCTION AND COORDINATION BY ELYSE M. ALLEN
DESIGN AND TYPESETTING BY BEVERLY JOEL, PULP, INK.
SEPARATIONS BY PROFESSIONAL GRAPHICS, ROCKFORD, IL
PRINTING AND BINDING BY CONTI TIPOCOLOR, FLORENCE, ITALY

PUBLISHING, THE ART INSTITUTE OF CHICAGO
KATIE REILLY, ASSOCIATE VICE PRESIDENT, PUBLISHING
LISA MEYEROWITZ, EDITORIAL DIRECTOR
LAUREN MAKHOLM, DIRECTOR OF PRODUCTION

IMAGING, THE ART INSTITUTE OF CHICAGO
BONNIE ROSENBERG, DIRECTOR OF IMAGING
NATHAN KEAY, ASSOCIATE DIRECTOR, PHOTOGRAPHY
ELYSE M. ALLEN, ASSOCIATE DIRECTOR, PRODUCTION

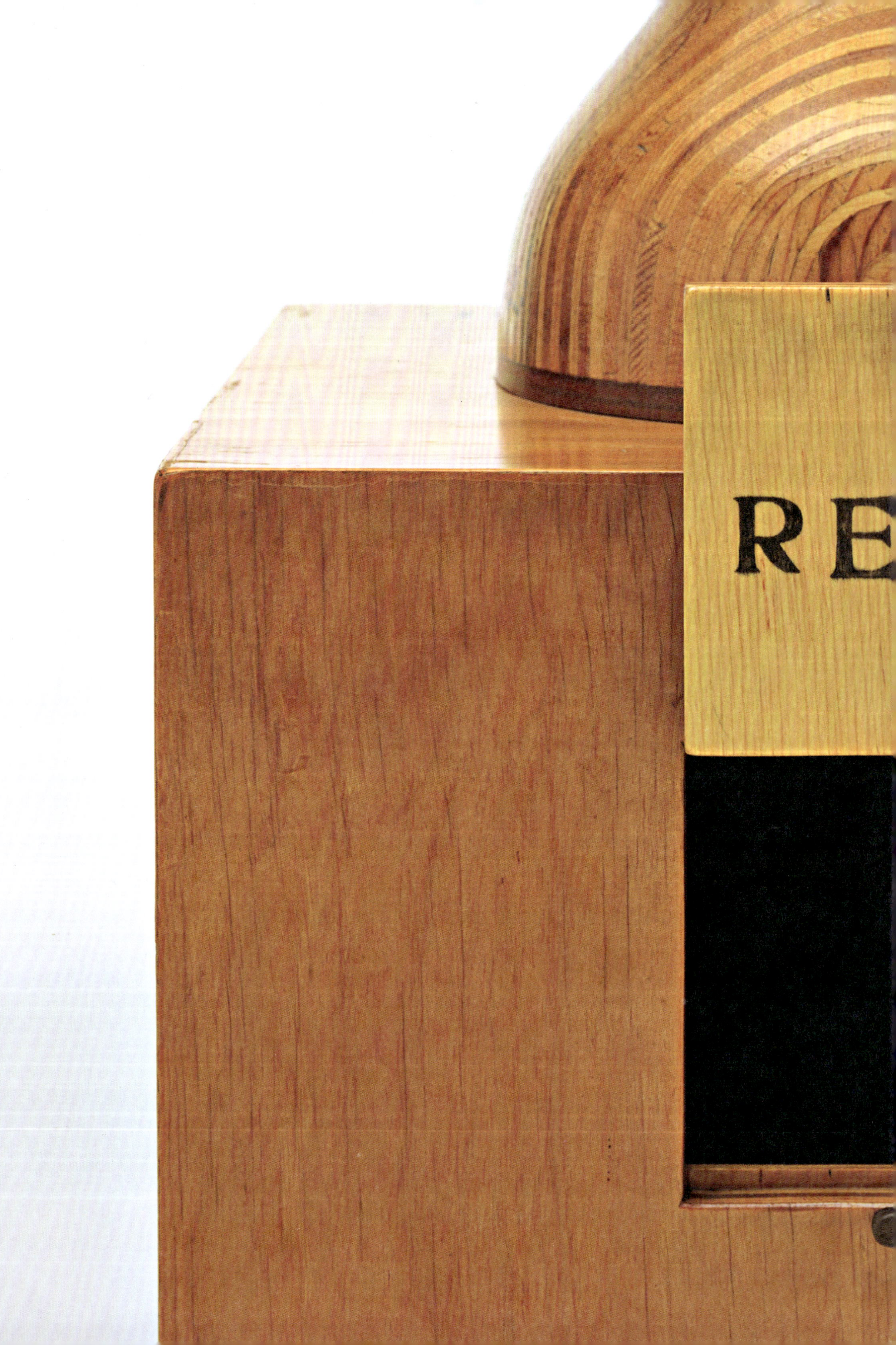
RE